Religion, Politics and Social Protest

Religion, Politics and Social Protest

Three Studies on Early Modern Germany

PETER BLICKLE
HANS-CHRISTOPH RUBLACK
WINFRIED SCHULZE

Edited by

Kaspar von Greyerz

With an Introduction by

Wolfgang J. Mommsen

THE GERMAN HISTORICAL INSTITUTE

London
GEORGE ALLEN & UNWIN
Boston Sydney

**George Allen & Unwin (Publishers) Ltd,
40 Museum Street, London WC1A 1LU, UK**

George Allen & Unwin (Publishers) Ltd,
Park Lane, Hemel Hempstead, Herts HP2 4TE, UK

Allen & Unwin, Inc.,
9 Winchester Terrace, Winchester, Mass. 01890, USA

George Allen & Unwin Australia Pty Ltd,
8 Napier Street, North Sydney, NSW 2060, Australia

First published in, 1984

British Library Cataloguing in Publication Data

Blickle, Peter
Religion, politics and social protest.
1. Reformation—Germany
I. Title II. Rublack, Hans Christoph
III. Schulze, Winfried
274.3'06 BR305.2
ISBN 0-04-940077-0

Library of Congress Cataloging in Publication Data

Blickle, Peter.
Religion, politics, and social protest.
Based on papers given in seminars at the German Historical Institute in 1980.
Includes bibliographical references and index.
1. Reformation—Germany—Addresses, essays, lectures.
2. Social movements—Germany—History—16th century—Addresses, essays, lectures. 3. Germany—Social conditions—Addresses, essays, lectures. 4. Germany—Politics and government—1517-1648—Addresses, essays, lectures.
I. Rublack, Hans-Christoph. II. Schulze, Winfried.
III. Greyerz, Kaspar von. IV. German Historical Institute of London.
BR307.B54 1984 943'.03 84-10963
ISBN 0-04-940077-0 (alk. paper)

Set in 11 on 13 point Garamond by V & M Graphics Ltd, Aylesbury and printed in Great Britain by Nene Litho and bound by Woolnough Bookbinding both of Wellingborough, Northants

Contents

Introduction

WOLFGANG J. MOMMSEN

The three studies by Peter Blickle, Hans-Christoph Rublack and Winfried Schulze collected in this volume have one theme in common, namely the social impact of the Reformation on German and other European societies in the sixteenth and seventeenth centuries. They represent important threads in current research in the Federal Republic of Germany on the social history of early modern Europe. The studies emerged from papers originally given in seminars at the German Historical Institute in 1980. While all three authors have published widely in German on the social history of the Reformation and German peasant revolts, British readers may not be as familiar with their work. Thus the German Historical Institute decided to publish these essays which provide a most informative insight into the views, research strategies and approaches currently dominant in the Federal Republic of Germany in this particular field of research. The German Historical Institute hopes to publish similar collections of essays on other topics of general interest in the near future; a collection of essays on the 'Holocaust' is currently in preparation. It is to be hoped that in this way the German Historical Institute can help to promote the co-operation between British and German historical research.

The essay by Peter Blickle on 'Social protest and Reformation theology' argues with much justification that the theology of the Reformation and the ideologies of the various social protest movements which began during that period had, in fact, much in common, whatever the theologians felt about it, and that one cannot be understood without the other. Blickle masterfully outlines an ideal-typical pattern of both urban and rural protest movements during the Reformation and points out in some detail how intimately connected they were to the theological teachings of the Reformation preachers. Social protest in its various forms was justified by contemporaries, albeit in very different ways, as based upon what they considered the only legitimate interpretation of the gospel. In this way Blickle succeeds in establishing a systematic link between the theology and the social protest movements of the time. Though in the end they were mostly suppressed, they made a lasting impact upon early modern society in Germany.

Hans-Christoph Rublack's essay on 'Political and social norms in urban communities in the Holy Roman Empire' tackles a wider theme, namely the fundamental norms of German society before and during the Reformation, that is to say, the value principles which not only legitimised the social fabric as such, but also served as guidelines for social action throughout. Rublack does so on a rather sophisticated, abstract level, relying to a considerable degree upon sociological conceptualisations. In a way, his theme is a corollary to Blickle's. He agrees with Blickle that the Reformation released enormous energies which tended to disrupt the traditional socio-political fabric of society, but he is concerned with the fact that most of the fundamental value norms of the age, particularly those with an 'integrative' content, did survive. These were invoked to preserve the cohesion of society in the face of disruptive forces. Rublack emphasises three of them, the ideas of *justice, peace* and *unity* (of the community or communities) which by and large remained valid norms, in this order, the upheavals of revolution notwithstanding. However, these norms were invoked in a highly flexible manner and indeed, were often referred to rather loosely, which made the principles appear virtually interchangeable and also useful for revolutionary action of various kinds. None the less, they continued to be used as guidelines in contemporary debates about the ideal social order and its legitimacy. Rublack attempts to demonstrate that these norms were not merely ideological, as people sincerely believed in them, though they were being put to various ideological uses. Though all this is presented on a fairly abstract level, it is supported by very interesting topical quotations from a wide variety of contemporary sources.

The essay by Winfried Schulze on 'Peasant resistance in Sixteenth- and Seventeenth-century Germany in a European context' covers a far wider field. In the first part of his essay Schulze gives a critical assessment of research both in the East and the West on the peasant protest movements in early modern Europe, and of the concepts and notions which provide the backbone of the analysis. In this context particular attention is given to Marxist approaches and to the advantages and shortcomings of analyses of peasant rebellions in terms of the Marxist concept of class struggle. Schulze suggests a structural-functional alternative which combines analysis on political and constitutional levels with analysis of the underlying long-term economic and social changes. Schulze then proceeds to present an ideal-typical explanatory model of peasant revolts in early modern Europe, concentrating on central and, to some degree, east-central Europe. He emphasises to begin with, that armed rebellion was but an extreme form of rural protest against the encroachment on the peasants' rights or traditional status by landlords, princes or the newly emerging governmental bureaucracies of the various regional states being formed in central Europe. Indeed, as he points out, a wide spectrum of forms of protest existed, mostly peaceful in nature, and only in specific cases erupting violently. Schulze suggests a triangular model of analysis for the peasants' revolts: the emerging institutional states' interest in suppressing ancient rights and practices and levying taxes in an orderly and efficient manner, thus destroying the remnants of the feudal order; the feudal or ecclesiastical landlords' interest in increasing their financial income from dues and tithes, thereby at times tending to push the exploitation of the rural population to unbearable limits; the peasants' interest in maintaining their ancient rights and traditions, while being allowed freely to participate in the exploitation of the opportunities provided by the agrarian market place. Schulze also makes a comparison between rural protest movements throughout Europe, with very interesting results. In general, revolts were most likely to occur only in those territories which were least advanced in economic terms, and in which the holder of governmental power was also the greatest, if not the only owner of landed property, while the mitigating forces of a modern governmental administration and/or traditional estates were largely lacking. On the whole, he succeeds in showing that given the circumstances, the great peasant uprisings particularly in southern Germany, were not merely irrational phenomena. Rather, they were caused by the coincidence of a variety of adverse factors. Indeed, the modern idea that all state power requires legitimation by the subjects derives in part from the theories of resistance against governmental or feudal violation of traditional rights developed among the peasant movements of early modern Europe.

None of these essays claims to cover the problems which they tackle in a comprehensive way. But they undoubtedly open up interesting lines of interpretation which may be fruitful for further research. They also provide the general reader with an informative presentation of many of the key issues around which present-day research in the social history of early modern Europe revolves. It is to be hoped that the fairly theoretical approach which these essays have in common and which, rightly or wrongly, may be considered as typically German, may be recognised as a useful way of mastering an immense field of historical data, rendering them meaningful in the light of the problems of our own times.

1

Social Protest and Reformation Theology

PETER BLICKLE

In a lecture he delivered in Washington in 1945 Thomas Mann tried to explain the roots of the demonic in the National Socialist regime to his American audience.[1] His views on the subject were subjective and intuitive, tied into a loose framework of causality, and he took frequent recourse to Luther. To Mann, Luther was both the personification of 'the Germanic' *par excellence* and in turn someone whose own social ethic and theology had effected a change in it. 'I would not like to have been Luther's dinner guest', Mann admitted, 'and am convinced I would have got on better with Leo X, the friendly humanist Luther called "the devil's pig - the Pope".' He added: 'The Germanic in its purest form - the separatist, anti-Roman, anti-European - alienates and frightens me even when it is presented as evangelical freedom and spiritual emancipation.'[2] Despite these critical lines, Mann obviously also admired Luther - the breaker of orthodox restraints, the creator of the national language, the musician. At the same time, however, Mann distances himself from Luther: 'He (Luther) was a heroic liberator ... but in the German mode, for he understood nothing of freedom. I am not talking about Christian liberty but about political freedom — the freedom of the citizens of a state. This concept did not just leave him cold, he despised the basic tenor and goals of such a notion from the bottom of his heart.' At the point at which theology and social protest intersect – Mann refers specifically to the Peasants' War – Luther stood in the way of progress. 'For the sad outcome of this first attempt at a German revolution', Mann continued, which 'could have given the entire course of German history a more fortunate turn towards Liberty, ... Luther, the man of the people, bears a good share of the responsibility.'[3]

Thomas Mann was certainly familiar with that interpretation of German history which holds the Reformation responsible for both social protest *and* its failure – indeed, charges Protestantism with having an abhorrence of revolution which renders it unfit for democracy.[4] It would, therefore, seem to be more of a necessity than just an interesting endeavour for the historian to undertake the task of evaluating the importance of the Reformation to German history by analysing the mutual dependence of Reformation theology and social protest. More precisely, the questions are these: (1) where and how is social protest articulated; (2) how does it stand in relationship to Reformation theology, and (3) what consequences arise from the possible combination of these two movements?[5] The inception of social protest during the Reformation period and the significance of Reformation theology for this protest become clear even from the most cursory perusal of the available source material. Below, three examples are offered which shed light on the suggested interrelationships.

In a petition of grievances addressed to the council of the imperial city of Frankfurt, the community makes numerous economic and social demands including: the removal of ground rents, abolition of excise taxes, a simplification of and reduction in administrative costs, communal use of the wooded areas, the abolition of certain other duties, and so on. These demands are tied to the following line of argument: 'Because we do owe more allegiance to God than to any mortal (Acts 5; 29) it is necessary that we abandon godless ways and begin to reform ourselves towards a godly, brotherly conduct, in praise of God the Almighty and the honour of His holy word, Christ our Lord, and for the promotion of brotherly unity.'[6] Having energetically demanded the abolition of serfdom, the removal of manorial dues and improvement in the administration of justice, a peasant petition from Upper Swabia ends

> It is our conclusion and opinion that if one or more of the here formulated articles should go against the Word of God, which we do not believe, that we reject that article if such can be proven to be the case in the Scriptures. If we are granted a particular article now which should later be proven to be unjust, we will abolish that article. Likewise, we reserve the right to make further demands should they be found to be justified in the Scriptures.[7]

In a joint mandate issued by the cities of Zürich, Bern and St Gallen regarding the Anabaptists, the following actions and beliefs are threatened with the punishment of death by drowning.[8]

> Although the Anabaptists are not the only ones who use the external water mark of re-baptism, they are nonetheless distinguishable by certain characteristics and features, namely that none of them carry a sword or sue for outstanding debts. They also say that no Christian, if he truly is one, should give or receive interest on capital, that all goods are free and should belong to the general community and that every person has property rights in them. They teach that no Christian should rule over another and are unabashed in doing so, having the audacity to base this claim on the Scriptures. And although government cannot be maintained without the bond and obligation of oath-swearing, all of them teach that a Christian should not swear an oath to the authorities or to anyone else – all of these things to the disgrace and oppression of Christian orderly government, brotherly love and general peace.

The selection of examples I have presented are – in a sense that we shall discuss later – representative. Consequently, we can develop a sharper line of questioning for the analysis of social protest: social protest originates in the urban and rural population.[9] Concrete economic and social demands are arranged within a vindicatory nexus with 'the Word of God' and 'the Gospel', the choice of words clearly denoting their origin in the Reformation, since both were logograms of contemporary Reformation theology. Apart from the distinction between urban and rural populations as agents of the protest where it existed, a two-fold type of protest can be discerned, which in short can be characterised as positive and negative protest. Positive protest ran via the Gospel from economic and social necessity towards a fairer and more just social and political order. Negative protest ran via the Gospel from social and political order and thus out of history. This description summarises the objective of the first section of this study which will look at the interaction between social protest and Reformation theology in a threefold approach; first, the urban movements, secondly, the peasant movements, and thirdly, the Anabaptist movement which extended over city and countryside. From there we shall attempt to draw conclusions about the significance of Reformation theology for social protest in the Reformation period.

In the case of the urban movements such an inquiry can rely on the broad basis of recent research which began with Bernd Moeller's investigations.[10] These have been expanded upon in examination of his thesis primarily in Anglo-Saxon research[11] – in this respect Arthur G. Dickens,[12] Steven Ozment,[13] Thomas Brady[14] and Robert Scribner[15] must be noted – and has culminated in the rather pointed thesis that the Reformation was an 'urban event'. This thesis appears to have gained support lately from the body of intensive German research on the nature of 'city and Reformation'.[16] Similarly wide in scope, but more controversial is the discussion of Anabaptism, which owes much of its impetus and findings to the efforts of Hans-Jürgen Goertz,[17] Claus Peter Clasen,[18] Gottfried Seebass[19] and Richard van Dülmen.[20] In contrast, however, the problem of the relationship between the Reformation and peasant protest has remained seriously unexplored in recent research. This situation is understandable in so far as the peasant revolt of 1525 has, until the accounts of Günther Franz[21] and Adolf Waas,[22] been too one-sidedly interpreted as the climax of peasant protest behaviour. Within the context of this problematic, the theme of 'Luther and the peasant revolt' adds little to the clarification of the issues to be discussed in the present study because it was usually employed apologetically in Luther's defence.[23] First steps towards exposing the interactionary relationship between Reformation and peasant revolt are evident in the works of Martin Brecht,[24] Justus Maurer,[25] and Heiko A. Oberman,[26] but so far the issue has been neither fully encompassed nor plausibly explained[27] – with the exception of the concept of the 'early bourgeois revolution'. This does tie the two movements together, but does so by using abstract constructions which jeopardise empirical verifiability.[28] Despite the obvious insights gained in recent years regarding the particular aspects I have mentioned, it must still be maintained, as Heiko A. Oberman has recently suggested, that the connections between specific forms of protest have not been clarified[29] and their relationship to Reformation theology has not been ascertained.[30]

I

Forms of what we are referring to here as *positive protest* are evident in the city (1) and in the countryside (2). The differences and similarities between them become clear if we develop a concentrated ideal-typical model of their progression.

(1) The urban protest movement of the Reformation[31] can

be divided into three phases.[32] The *first phase* is introduced by the sermon of the preacher. This begins with a critique of the papacy, moves on to a critique of the monastic and secular clergy, then on to questioning the position of the old church on basic matters and finally on into the social sphere. Accusations of injustice on the part of the authorities and the questioning of tithes both belong to the general repertoire of the preacher. The end point of this critical sermon is rejection of the church's dogmatic tradition in favour of the 'pure' Gospel. The forum is a continually growing and progressively more agitated community. Opposition comes, naturally enough, from those under attack – the urban monasteries and clergy – and they have outside support from the hierarchically structured church in the person of the bishops. So the city councils fall prey to double pressure, from within and from without. Should the council adopt this critique and translate it into political action – even compromise is still possible at this stage – social protest would be headed off and the transition towards Reformation initiated.

Should the council not do so, it is possible, though not a necessary result, that the protest will enter the *second phase.* This is characterised by the interference in these tensions of one section of the community, or of individual guilds. Passive resistance is articulated in the refusal to pay dues to the monasteries and the old church tithes, or active opposition leads to the formation of communal, pro-Reformation committees. Active opposition is accompanied by concrete demands. These are primarily social and political in nature, occasionally also economic, and reflect a frequently longer-standing accumulation of grievances. They call for the dissolution of the monasteries and communal incorporation of the clergy, abolition of the mass and the introduction of the 'pure' Gospel as the exclusive reference in preaching. The position of the council is considerably weaker in this second phase than in the first. Its authority and legitimation show clear symptoms of decline: the means of existence of the city's charitable organisations (the hospitals) is acutely threatened by the refusal to pay tithes. Within the possible range of reactions, which can be roughly divided into co-operation, compromise or resistance, only the first offers a real opportunity for heading off the revolt. Neither compromise, still less energetic opposition, can pacify the agitated community.

Thus, in the *third phase* the inner-city protest movement crystallises into revolt. Demands are made for the removal of old-faith councillors or for the expansion of the council, which can no longer claim to be the representative organ of the community. Enforcement of these demands involves the threat of military force, violent attacks on adherents of the old faith - usually the clergy - and iconoclastic riots. A religious debate between the old and reformed clergy over the issue of correct belief ensues, the outcome of which is predetermined by the community's claim to competency in matters of religious doctrine. As a rule, the result of this third phase is the introduction of the Reformation and it is often coupled with constitutional change. Whereas most of the reformatory gains will be retained, this is not true of most of the constitutional revisions.

(2) A model of the development of rural protest[33] can likewise be divided into three phases. The *first phase* is characterised by peasant assemblies and the drafting of local grievances. The contents of these can be very generally summarised here as a critique of feudalism along traditional lines of argument.

The authorities' unwillingness to abandon a tactic of delay in favour of a realistic handling of these complaints prompts a *second phase* of interregional alliances and the drafting of regional grievances. These incorporate the local grievances and bring them into the context of a common cause, which - and this is decisive to the line of questioning in this study - gives the local grievances a new sense of legitimacy and enlarges their material scope. The grievances are legitimised by 'divine law', the 'Word of God' and 'the Gospel': they are expanded to include a demand for communal election of ministers and the preaching of the pure Gospel. The reformers are assigned the responsibility of judging the compatibility of the demands with the 'divine law' of the Gospel and they, like the feudal upper classes, deny the peasants' claim to the Gospel as the normative category for ordering the secular sphere.

A peasantry made insecure in this manner generally divides into a reformist and a radical camp and, through the formation of the latter, rural protest enters its *third phase*. Short-term rule of the 'common man' is installed as monasteries and castles are stormed and a constitution is conceived out of the power vacuum, establishing the insurgents as the natural conveyors of authoritative functions. The 'common weal' and 'brotherly Christian love' are presented as the ethical maxims, and the community fills the necessary positions by holding elections. The military defeat of the insurgents by the feudal upper classes coincides with this process of reconstruction.

Common to both forms of positive protest is the repeated and argumentative invocation of the Gospel with a clear emphasis on the New Testament. It provides the basis for urban and rural anticlericalism, with its cutting-edge against the monasteries and orthodox clergy; it legitimises the demand for communal autonomy, exemplified in the call for the right to decide issues of correct religious doctrine, to elect the minister and to allocate tithes; and it is ultimately made the yardstick of social and political order. The latter occurs, though only vaguely at first, when the emphasis on 'common weal' versus the *grosse Hansen* is coupled with the deduction taken from the Bible that an increase in brotherliness and charity is essential to social and political order and that further communal prerogatives are indispensable to ensure the implementation of these demands.

Beyond these similarities the Gospel was accorded differing emphasis in the city and countryside. Economic demands were less extensive in the city. Given the fundamental acceptance of the basic tenets of the city's constitution, the political perspectives were exhausted with the replacement or increase in the number of persons holding public office. As an aid in evaluating the significance of this, it may be helpful to point out that the urban revolts of the sixteenth century are less significant from a constitutional point of view than the guild struggles of the fourteenth century.[34]

Rural society's invocation of the Gospel had more far-reaching economic and political consequences. As an alternative to the traditional legitimation of grievances through reference to the 'old order' (*Altes Herkommen*), it permitted the formulation of demands which could not have been justified through allusion to that 'old order' – such as the abolition of serfdom. Taken as an indisputable, this-wordly principle of order, it expels all those from the socio-political association who refuse to recognise the Gospel as this principle. Rural society uses the ideological apparatus of Reformation theology in striving to create a political form of constitutionality rooted in communal autonomy and thus to approximate the constitutional forms of the city.

(3) Just as there could not have been positive social protest in the 'Reformation period' without its having absorbed and digested Reformation thought, so there could not have been negative protest devoid of this influence. Bearing in mind that the *exodus from history* was never a mass phenomenon and therefore remained largely tied to individual personalities it is also difficult to establish an ideal-typical model in the case of the Anabaptists.

This much can, none the less, be extracted from the diffuse body of empirical data: Anabaptism, in its *first phase* insisted on the radical reorganisation of the ministry and church tax system for ensuring the implementation of the Gospel, thereby separating itself from the majority of leading Reformation theologians, who were prepared to compromise on those issues, and simultaneously antagonising both reformers and the secular authorities.

The Anabaptists were too few in number to effect an opposition comparable to the city or peasant movements, so that in a *second phase* of hardening standpoints on both sides, withdrawal from social and political order seemed the only option open to them for rescuing their cause. Indeed, at this point the path of Anabaptism forks off in two directions: the first route entails the Anabaptists' withdrawal from the city council and a separation in custom and life-style. This goes hand in hand with the development of their theology which, in reaching back into the New Testament *ecclesia*, defines the Christian community as a persecuted and suffering minority. At the end of this route lies their complete refusal to co-operate with the authorities whether in matters of civil defence or armed service, judicial or administrative functions. This renunciation found more than symbolic expression in their opposition to the oath of allegiance – a dramatic act for the sixteenth century.[35].

The second route entails steadfast adherence to the radical and original proclamation of the total reversal of the secular order offered in Müntzer's line of thinking – living and organising itself in expectation of God's final judgement over the godless. This branch of Anabaptism is characterised by a belief in the advent of the *eschaton* and the ascertainability of the exact date of this event, revealing itself precisely as an exodus from this world. This date was derived from an acrobatic numbers mystique and had to be revised several times, watering down the certainty to vague hopefulness.

No matter which route the Anabaptists went, they were persecuted mercilessly by the authorities, the established Roman church and by the upcoming new church. Bernd Moeller describes this situation in the suggestive formulation: 'the scorners of the world experienced the scorn of the world.'[36] Threatened with the death penalty, introduced at the imperial diet of 1529, they fled increasingly to the borders of the Empire: to the Netherlands and Moravia.

The question remains as to how positive and negative protest are related. The methodical approach to clarifying this is to position social protest along a time axis. Urban disturbances can be ascertained in the period from 1522 to 1535,[37] rural disturbances between 1523 and 1526,[38] and the protest of the Anabaptists as a wider movement from 1525 to 1534 –5.[39] As far as the time element is concerned, this amounts to a succession of urban, rural and Anabaptist movements. The decisive question is whether chronological succession is the result of a causal dependence. Here one would have to answer in the affirmative. Research on the Peasants' War has established convincingly that the components of Reformation theology were carried from the city into the countryside: Alsatians could – and did – call on Bucar, Zell and Capito, the peasants of the Black Forest on Hubmaier, the Upper Swabians on Schappeler, and the Thuringians on Müntzer. Recent research has also put the noticeable spread of Anabaptism after 1525 into a convincing causal connection with the Peasants' War. Gottfried Seebass has noted close regional and personal ties between the two movements in Franconia[40] and James Stayer has shown a similar relationship in Switzerland.[41] To the extent that Anabaptism in general has been examined, as recently by Martin Haas,[42] Richard van Dülmen[43] and Hans Jürgen Goertz,[44] the peasant revolt is considered very important to the Anabaptist movement. Any criticism of this view which has arisen so far has been based on the argument that the Anabaptists were, in many regions, recruited primarily from the city.[45] The contradiction, apparently inherent in a correlation of urban disturbances, peasant revolt and Anabaptism, dissolves when one realises that the very experience of transforming Reformation theology into political practice was a necessary pre-condition of Anabaptist, negative protest. In which case, indeed, it makes sense that the movement inherited those elements of the urban population which had experienced the failure of the concept of radical Reformation in the city.

It is not difficult to see that positive and negative social protest arise from the same theological patrimony. The

Gospel, understood as the 'pure' doctrine after the elimination of the previously binding dogmatic tradition, retains an axiomatic character from which all subsequent derivatives become self-evident. Included in these are the autonomy of the faithful and the concepts of community and charity. All forms of social protest in the Reformation period can be characterised and qualified as being essentially attempts at making the 'idea' 'practical', as seeking a direct translation of Reformation theology into political and social behaviour. Was this a legitimate extension of the disposition of Reformation theologians?

II

Although the theologies of the reformers are many-sided and operate on different levels, they do reveal their shared tendencies in their initial separation from the teaching of the old church. The most important of these shared tenets could be said to be: the justification by God's grace (*sola gratia*) through man's faith (*sola fide*) as revealed in the Gospel as the Word of God (*sola scriptura*), whereby the power of the ecclesiastical sacraments to convey salvation and grace is annulled. Taking faith to be grounds for justification by God implies the equality of all believers and flows consequently into the *priesthood of all believers*, whereby the hierarchical order of the church is annulled. Taking the Gospel to be the faith-inspiring Word of God elevates the Scriptures to the position of 'centre-piece' of all theology but, in turn, results in the negation of the church's 'dogma' (whereby the church is relieved of its doctrinal authority). The new church which is competing with the old hierarchically structured Roman church becomes a *communal church*.[46]

In the process of making this theology more concrete the reformers naturally ran into opposition from the established Roman church which was all the less willing to compromise because it was being existentially threatened. It fought the Reformation movement with all the force available to it as the established church and secular power in the person of the ecclesiastical princes. This resulted in innumerable political conflicts on which the reformers were forced to take a stand.

How did the reformers solve such problems? They were certainly not wanting in political views: Zwingli opted for a campaign of all reformed forces against the Catholic Habsburgs, Müntzer for the expulsion and execution of the territorial princes of central Germany, and Luther for the transformation of the lands controlled by the Teutonic Order into the secular principality. All of these views transcend the judicial framework in which the late Middle Ages were used to thinking or arguing. These are clearly breaches of law and revolutionary acts that are being propagated and/or put into action. How do the reformers legitimise them?

How *Zwingli* developed and justified his political views can be shown in brief from a look at his interpretation of the role of the authorities. Zwingli proceeds from the assumption that it is the function of the authorities to punish wrongdoers and protect the innocent. That is the 'Will of God'. It follows, according to Zwingli, that 'the laws of the authorities should therefore be of the same kind as the Will of God'.[47] The Will of God, taken by Zwingli to be the normative foundation for governmental legislation and thereby for political order, reveals itself in 'the law God gave'. He describes this God-given law, or 'divine justice' more closely:

> Note briefly: all laws regarding our fellow man should be founded in the law of nature. Do unto others as you would others do unto you, Matt. 7. Matthew expressed this in even clearer words, Matt. 22: 'Love thy neighbour as thyself.' If a law is contrary to this Word of God then it is against God.

Zwingli would not have been a reformer had he believed that

the existing forms of government were primarily Christian in this sense. Consequently, he had the problem of deciding what would have to happen if the secular order did not correspond to the natural and God-given law as defined by himself. His answer is plain and to the point: 'all old laws' must be examined in essence 'as to whether or not they conform to the God-given law of brotherly love and nature – these being one law'. Zwingli envisages here a renewal of the state through its christianisation. The Christianity of the authorities is not just desirable, it is imperative. The new political order is being legitimised by the Gospel. The methodological means of ascertaining this political order is biblical exegesis.

It is also *Müntzer's* intention to actualise the will of God. This, however, can be brought about only by believers, since only they know God's will. Faith stems from the experience of the cross.[48] One must allow oneself to be crucified with Christ, must bear the cross, must divest oneself of human nature and creatureliness. This is the prerequisite for experiencing the 'Spirit' of God and the experience through which one becomes *christusförmig* (Christ-like). Through the experience of the cross and spirit one becomes justified by God. For Müntzer the world is divided into 'the elect' and 'the godless' – into those who have, deservedly, the correct faith and those who, being undeserving, do not. With the category of 'election' Müntzer sets out along the momentous path of his theory of the organisation of the secular sphere.

The 'elect' know God's will because they have become Christ-like. They therefore become the executors of his will, a role that Müntzer essentially interprets as preparing the world for the coming of Christ. This means the godless must be destroyed. The princes come under the verdict of 'godless' in any case, because they refuse to raise their sword on behalf of the chosen, the sword having been given to them by God for just this purpose. So it must be taken away from them and given to the 'elect' to carry out God's will. Accordingly, Müntzer's concept of revolution proves to be a derivative of his theology. The methodological process for justifying the right of resistance follows, by deduction, from his over-all system of theological speculation.

Luther was frequently asked by communities and city councils to explain how the legal barriers to the introduction of the Reformation could be overcome. He gave clear guidelines as early as 1523 in his pamphlet, 'That a Christian assembly or community has the right and the power to judge all teaching, to extend calls to teachers, appoint or dismiss them based on, and originating in the Bible.' In it he says: in order to 'judge teaching and appoint or dismiss teachers and preachers, one must not rely on human laws, rights, tradition, custom, habit, etc., no matter if, God willing, it be decreed by pope or emperor, prince or bishop, or been employed in half the world or the whole world, or in effect for one or a thousand years.'[49] This position, which casts off the thousand years of judicial tradition, is developed from the letter to the Thessalonians; that is, it is derived from the Bible. *Eike Wolgast* summarised Luther's and the Wittenberg theologians' position on political conflict thus: they applied the *sola scriptura*-principle to daily political life and called on reason only in a subsidiary way – only in so far as doing so substantiated the information offered by the Scriptures.[50]

The few references to Zwingli's, Müntzer's and Luther's views about the secular sphere make clear – and this is essential to the context of our theme – that the Bible is taken to be the standard, and the deductive exegetical process the method employed, in solving this-worldly problems.

Social protest during the Reformation period used the same modes of argument that the reformers used on the rostrum, from the pulpit, or in pamphlets. The Bible as the standard and exegesis as method are the two principles with which Reformation theology and social protest faced the world they found. From this point of view it is by no means mandatory that one accept the reformers' thesis of the 'rendering into flesh'. In his 'Admonition to peace in response to the Twelve

Articles of the peasantry',[51] Luther accused the peasants 'of making Christian freedom entirely that of the flesh', using the Gospel as an excuse 'to exercise their wantonness and seek their fortune there.' Zwingli shared this view in principle[52] and Müntzer explained the failure of his revolutionary campaign by stating 'that each sought his own personal profit more than the justification of Christendom.'[53]

Ever since, forms of social protest have been discredited to the point where the 'common man' is derided as having had 'lower' motives for action in cases where he did participate in introducing the Reformation. This view has even been stylised into a theorem, which is supported by the prescholarly conviction that the 'common man' misunderstood the reformers' intention.[54] One must be permitted to ask whether social protest could not be better characterised as congeniality, finality and consistency: congenial to Reformation theology in the sense that the Gospel was adopted as the normative principle; final in the sense that the Gospel was made the imperative for the entire worldly sphere; and consistent in the sense that all forms of social protest sought to establish the same principles – autonomy of the individual, community as the principle of socio-political organisation, and the common weal as the ethical legitimation of human existence.

To qualify social protest as being society's legitimate interpretation of the Reformation seems all the more justified because the formulations of the theologians, departing from a common reformatory objective and the transformation of theology into ethic through the Reformation itself led to entirely different results. Where can one still see the similarities between the former 'fellow travellers' Luther and Müntzer in their concrete theologies when we have 'devotional theology' on the one hand and 'theology of revolution' on the other? Or where between the old friends Zwingli and Grebel? The broad spectrum of Protestantism ranging from an ascetic, combative, world-changing Calvinism to a quietist German Lutheranism shows what can become of the same theological approach in the dialectical confrontation with secular order.

The programmatic point made by Heiko A. Oberman referring specifically only to the Peasants' War, and one which is yet to be elaborated upon here – that social protest 'can claim its place in church history with the same right as the movements coming out of Wittenberg, Geneva or Trent'[55] – can be supported and given more precision by adding that the fact that they can claim this 'place' is determined by the categories mentioned earlier of congeniality, finality and consistency. Any attempt to reduce social protest to egoism motivated by economic interests is rendered untenable by the fact that the insurgents risked their existence and their very lives for the 'secularisation' (*Verweltlichung*) of the Reformation.

III

Social protest unleashed regressive powers in the empire and, indeed, had to since it aimed at actualising in the worldly sphere the same things Reformation theology wanted to bring about in the ecclesiastical and spiritual spheres. Some of this was achieved: formulated in negative terms, the destruction of the hierarchically structured global church, and in positive terms, the emphasis on the dignity of man through his immediacy to God, and the resultant implications, such as communal autonomy or the priesthood of all believers. Social protest is symmetrically related to this. Formulated negatively, its objective was to destroy feudal structures; formulated positively, it sought to expand communal competency (all the way to autonomy) and extend the political rights of the individual.

The subsequent history of the Reformation and political developments in the empire – the narrow ecclesiastical sphere need not be considered here – cannot be understood unless one understands the prior fusion of Reformation theology and social protest. Since the legitimacy of the feudal order was put into question by this social protest, if not in fact attacked, sheer survival instinct forced the princes and the nobility to try and separate social protest from Reformation theology, in order to prevent fundamental structural changes in the political order. A general repression of the Reformation seemed too dangerous if the desire was to avoid a *da capo* of the uprisings. The imperial diets of 1526 and 1529 repeatedly expressed this fear. The only remaining option was to bring the Reformation under state control. This happened in the favour bestowed on the Wittenberg version of the Reformation, not the Zürich or Strasbourg versions. Zwingli and Bucar pressed for the Christianisation of the political order as well, while Luther always accorded the authorities their historical prerogatives: their Christianity was something desirable, not something mandatory. It is no coincidence that the Zürich Reformation, which initially enjoyed considerable support in Upper Germany, was driven out of the empire and that Strasbourg, with its urban satellites, was forced to assimilate itself along Wittenberg lines. In this way, the Reformation within the empire found its manifold original perspectives reduced and politically neutralised. The comprehensive *reformatio* as ecclesiastical and secular new order had failed.

Notes : Chapter 1

1 Thomas Mann, *Reden und Aufsätze*, Vol. iii, *Gesammelte Werke*, Vol. xi (Berlin and Frankfurt, 1960), pp. 1126–48.

2 ibid., pp. 1132–33.

3 ibid., p. 1134.

4 Reference is made selectively to a few representative views which point in this direction: K. Barth, *Eine Schweizer Stimme 1938–1945* (Zollikon-Zürich, 1945), pp. 14 and 113. M. Scheler, 'Von zwei deutschen Krankheiten', in Scheler, *Schriften zur Soziologie und Weltanschauungenslehre*, 2nd edn (Bern, 1963), pp. 204–19. J. Burckhardt, *Historische Fragmente* (Stuttgart-Berlin, 1942), pp. 90–1. M. Weber, *Wirtschaft und Gesellschaft: Grundrisse der verstehenden Soziologie*, 5th edn (Tübingen, 1972), p. 287. (In English G. Roth and C. Wittich (eds),

Economy and Society: an Outline of Interpretive Sociology, 2 vols, Berkeley, Los Angeles and London, 1978).

5 This study is limited to German-speaking areas. I am considering a more extensive and more differentiated analysis to correlate certain theological orientations with the nature and progress (*Verlaufsformen*) of social protest. I wish to thank Professor Bernd Moeller (Göttingen) and Dr Robert W. Scribner (Cambridge) for their critical reading of this study and their valuable suggestions.

6 Akademie der Wissenschaften der DDR, general ed., *Flug-Schriften der Bauernkriegszeit*, ed. A. Laube and H. W. Seiffert (Berlin-East, 1975), pp. 59–65. The citation is from p. 59. Original text: 'Dieweyl wir nun Gott mehr dan den menschen zu gehorsamen schuldig (Apg 5,29), ist hoch von nôtten, das wir daz gotloß wesen faren lassen und ein gôtlich, brüderlich handelung, Gott dem almechtigen zu lobe und eren seines heyligen worts, Christi unsers hern und zu fôrderung brüderlicher eynikeyt, anfahen unß selbst zu reformieren.'

7 G. Franz (ed.), *Quellen zur Geschichte des Bauernkrieges*, (Munich, 1963), pp. 178–9. Original text: 'Zum zwelften ist unser Beschluß und endliche Mainung, wann ainer oder mer Artikel, alhie gestelt, so dem Wort Gotes nit gemeß weren, als wir dann nit vermainen, dieselbigen Artikel wol man uns mit dem Wort Gots für unzimlich anzaigen, wolt wir darvon abston, wann mans uns mit Grund der Schrift erklert. Ob man uns schon etlich Artikel jetz zuließ und hernach sich befend, das Unrecht weren, sollen si von Stund an tot und absein, nichts mer gelten. Dergleichen ob sich in der Schrift mit der Warhait mer Artikel erfunden, die wider Got und Beschwernus des Nächsten weren, wöll wir uns auch vorbehalten und beschlossen haben.'

8 H. Fast (ed.), *Quellen zur Geschichte der Täufer in der Schweiz*, Vol. ii: Ostschweiz (Zürich, 1973), pp. 1–7. The citation is from pp. 3–4. Original text: 'Item wiewol sy [the Anabaptists] nit all das eüsserlich wasserzaichen deß widertauffs gebrauchen, so seind sy doch mit annderen zaichen und brandtmalen verzaichnet und beschruwen, namlich das kainer kain tegen tragen noch sein außstendig schulden mit recht und gericht einbringen sölle. Sy halten und sagen auch, das kain christ vom andern, so er annderst ain christ sein wöll, kain zins noch gült umb ainicherlay hauptgůt weder geben noch nemen soll, das auch alle zeytliche gůter frey und gemeyn und yeder volkomne aigenschafft dartzů haben mög ... Item sy halten und leren on alles entsitzen, vermessen sich auch mit hailger schrifft zů erhalten, das kain christ kain oberer sein mög. Und wiewol die oberkait on die pflicht und das band dess ayds nit erhallten werden noch bestand haben mag, so leren und halten sy doch on all sündrung und underschaid, das kain christ kain ayd (auch der oberkait) unnd sunst nyemandts thůn noch schwören solle, alles zů schmach und verdruckung christenlicher und ordenlicher oberkait, brůderlicher lieb und gemains fridens.'

9 The third social group that might have reacted to the Reformation in protest was the lower nobility. The activities of this group were essentially exhausted after Franz von Sickingen's feud with the prince-electorate of Trier, which differed substantially from other forms of protest in its limited congeniality toward the Reformation message. Regarding the diversity of responses to the Reformation among the nobility, see B. Moeller, *Deutschland in Zeitalter der Reformation*, Deutsche Geschichte, Vol. iv (Göttingen, 1977), pp. 80 ff., and V. Press, 'Adel,

Reich und Reformation', in W. J. Mommsen (ed.), *Stadtbürgertum und Adel in der Reformation: Studien zur Sozialgeschichte der Reformation in England und Deutschland*, Veröffentlichungen des Deutschen Historischen Instituts London, Vol. v (Stuttgart, 1979), pp. 330–83.

10 B. Moeller, *Reichstadt und Reformation*, Schriften des Vereins für Reformationsgeschichte, no. 180 (Gütersloh, 1962). (In English *Imperial Cities and the Reformation: Three Essays*, trans. and ed. H. C. E. Midelfort and M. U. Edwards, Philadelphia, 1972).

11 B. Hall, 'The Reformation city', *Bulletin of the John Rylands Library*, lvi (1971), 103–48.

12 A. G. Dickens, *The German Nation and Martin Luther*, (London, 1974).

13 S. E. Ozment, *The Reformation in the Cities: the Appeal of Protestantism to Sixteenth Century Germany and Switzerland*, (New Haven, Conn. and London, 1975).

14 T. A. Brady, jun., *Ruling Class, Regime and Reformation at Strasbourg, 1520–1555*, Studies in Medieval and Reformation Thought, Vol. xxii (Leiden, 1978).

15 Most recently R. W. Scribner, 'Reformation, carnival and the world turned upside-down', in I. Bátori (ed.), *Städtische Gesellschaft und Reformation*, Kleine Schriften, Vol. ii, Spätmittelalter und Frühe Neuzeit: Beiträge zur Geschichtsforschung, Vol. xii (Stuttgart, 1980), pp. 234–64.

16 In this field the leading historians in more recent German research are Hans-Christoph Rublack, Erdmann Weyrauch, Ingrid Bátori, Heinz Schilling and Wilfried Ehbrecht. See the recently published collective volumes containing further bibliographical references to the work of the authors above: I. Bátori (ed.), *Städtische Gesellschaft und Reformation* (see n. 15). F. Petri (ed.), *Kirche und gesellschaftlicher Wandel in deutschen und niederländischen Städten der werdenden Neuzeit*, Städteforschung, Reihe A, Vol. 10 (Cologne and Vienna, 1980); W. J. Mommsen (ed.), *Stadtbürgertum und Adel in der Reformation* (see n. 9).

17 H.-J. Goertz (ed.), *Umstrittenes Täufertum, 1525–1975: Neue Forschungen*, (Göttingen, 1975). Goertz, *Die Täufer: Geschichte und Deutung*, (Munich, 1980).

18 C.-P. Clasen, *The Anabaptists in South and Central Germany, Switzerland and Austria* (Ithaca, NY and London, 1978).

19 G. Seebass, 'Bauernkrieg und Täufertum in Franken', *Zeitschrift für Kirchengeschichte*, lxxxv (1974), 284–300.

20 R. van Dülmen, *Reformation als Revolution: Soziale Bewegung und religiöser Radikalismus in der deutschen Reformation*, dtv, Wissenschaftliche Reihe, no. 4273 (Munich, 1977).

21 G. Franz, *Der deutsche Bauernkrieg*, 10th edn (Darmstadt, 1975).

22 A. Waas, *Die Bauern im Kampf um Gerechtigkeit 1300–1525*, 2nd edn (Munich, 1976).

23 See, for instance, P. Althaus, *Luthers Haltung im Bauernkrieg* (Libelli 2), 4th edn (Darmstadt, 1971). F. Lütge, 'Luthers Eingreifen in den Bauernkrieg in seinen sozialgeschichtlichen Voraussetzungen und Auswirkungen', *Jahrbücher für Nationalökonomie und Statistik*, clviii (1943), esp. 372 and 389–90.

24 M. Brecht, 'Der theologische Hintergrund der Zwölf Artikel der Bauernschaft in

Schwaben von 1525: Christoph Schappelers und Sebastian Lotzers Beitrag', *Zeitschrift für Kirchengeschichte*, lxxxv (1974), 174–208.

25 J. Maurer, *Prediger im Bauernkrieg*, Calwer Theologische Monographien, Vol. v (Stuttgart, 1979).

26 H. A. Oberman, 'Tumultus rusticorum: Vom "Klosterkrieg" zum Fürstensieg. Beobachtungen zum Bauernkrieg unter besonderer Berücksichtigung zeitgenössischer Beurteilungen', *Zeitschrift für Kirchengeschichte*, lxxxv (1974), 301–16. (In English 'The gospel of social unrest', in R. Scribner and G. Benecke (eds), *The German Peasant War of 1525 – New Viewpoints*, London, 1979, pp. 39–51).

27 First results will be available in the forthcoming doctoral thesis (University of Saarbrücken) of Francisca Conrad, *Die Rezeption der reformatorischen Theologie in der ländlichen Gesellschaft des Elsass*. See also my own attempt in P. Blickle, *Die Revolution von 1525*, 2nd edn (Munich and Vienna, 1981), pp. 237–44. (In English *The Revolution of 1525: German Peasants' War from a New Perspective*, trans. T. A. Brady, jun., and H. C. E. Midelfort, Baltimore, Md and London, 1981).

28 For a summary of the older discussion, cf. R. Wohlfeil (ed.), *Reformation oder frühbürgerliche Revolution?*, nymphenburger texte zur wissenschaft, Vol. v (Munich, 1972), esp. R. Wohlfeil's introduction, pp. 7–41. The more recent debate can essentially be found in G. Heitz *et al.* (eds), *Der Bauer im Klassenkampf: Studien zur Geschichte des deutschen Bauernkrieges und der bäuerlichen Klassenkämpfe im Spätfeudalismus* (Berlin-East, 1975), and in G. Brendler and A. Laube (eds), *Der deutsche Bauernkrieg 1524/25: Geschichte – Tradition – Lehren*, Akademie der Wissenschaften der DDR: Schriften des Zentralinstituts für Geschichte, Vol. lvii (Berlin-East, 1977).

29 H. A. Oberman, *Werden und Wertung der Reformation: Vom Wegestreit zum Glaubenskampf* (Tübingen, 1977), esp. pp. 372–6. (In English *Masters of the Reformation: the Emergence of a New Intellectual Climate in Europe*, trans. D. Martin, Cambridge, 1981).

30 ibid., p. 378: 'Der wertende Alleingang des Theologen genauso wie derjenige des Sozial- und Verfassungshistorikers scheidet als legitime Form der Geschichtsschreibung aus.' For a similar view, see also K. H. zur Mühlen, 'Luther zwischen Tradition und Revolution: Probleme gegenwärtiger Lutherforschung', *Luther*, xlvii (1976), 61–76.

31 To avoid misunderstanding I should point out that the theme of city and Reformation is not at issue here, but rather only one segment of that larger topic.

32 The development of individual city reformations, which differ widely from case to case, has not yet been presented in the form of a comprehensive model. This certainly has something to do with the difficulties involved in systematising the available data. The outline presented here relies essentially on the literature cited in n. 16.

33 This is developed from the material in G. Franz's research, see n. 21.

34 This general statement has recently been reconfirmed in the collective volume edited by W. Ehbrecht, *Städtische Führungsgruppen und Gemeinde in der werdenden Neuzeit*, Städteforschung, Reihe A, Vol. ix (Cologne and Vienna, 1980).

35 H. Fast (as in n. 8), pp. 31–2. For the importance of the oath for sixteenth-

century society, see Saarbrücker Arbeitsgruppe, 'Huldigungseid und Herrschaftsstruktur im Hattgau (Elsass)', in *Jahrbuch für westdeutsche Landesgeschichte*, vi (1980), 117–55.

36 B. Moeller (as in n. 9), p. 104. For the developmental model outlined here, see literature cited in nn. 17–20.

37 cf. B. Moeller (as in n. 9), p. 111.

38 This includes agrarian unrest in Switzerland. For the chronology, see G. Franz (as in n. 21).

39 H. A. Oberman (as in n. 29) recently dated the beginning of the Anabaptist movement in Zürich as being in 1523.

40 In his opinion there is no doubt, 'dass das Hutsche Täufertum seine Anhänger in Franken vornehmlich bei den früheren Aufständischen suchte und fand', see G. Seebass (as in n. 19), 229.

41 A. Stayer, 'Die Anfänge des schweizerischen Täufertums im reformierten Kongregationalismus', in H.-J. Goertz (ed.), *Umstrittenes Täufertum* (as in n. 17), pp. 19–49.

42 M. Haas, 'Der Weg der Täufer in die Absonderung', in H.-J. Goertz (ed.), *Umstrittenes Täufertum*, (as in n. 17), pp. 50–78.

43 R. van Dülmen (as in n. 20), p. 175.

44 H.-J. Goertz, *Die Täufer* (as in n. 17).

45 B. Moeller (as in n. 9), p. 104.

46 See the summary by G. Ebeling, 'Luther', in *Die Religion in Geschichte und Gegenwart*, Vol. iv, 3rd edn (Tübingen, 1960), pp. 495–520, and R. Stupperich, *Die Reformation in Deutschland*, dtv, no. 3202 (Munich, 1972), pp. 42 ff.

47 The following examples refer to article 39 of Zwingli's 'Auslegung der Schlussreden', following O. Frei, *Zwingli, der Verteidiger des Glaubens*, pt 2: Auslegung und Begründung der Schlussreden (Zürich, 1952), pp. 112–23. For the connection between theology and ethics, see also the discussion in G. W. Locher, 'Grundzüge der Theologie Huldrych Zwinglis im Vergleich mit derjenigen Martin Luthers und Johannes Calvins in Locher, *Huldrych Zwingli in neuer Sicht: Zehn Beiträge zur Theologie der Zürcher Reformation* (Zürich and Stuttgart, 1969), pp. 173–270, republished in revised form in Locher, *Die Zwinglische Reformation im Rahmen der europäischen Kirchengeschichte* (Göttingen, 1979), pp. 197–225.

48 Müntzer unfolds his 'theology of revolution' primarily in his writings published in 1524. See G. Franz (ed.), *Thomas Müntzer: Schriften und Briefe; Kritische Gesamtausgabe*, Quellen und Forschungen zur Reformationsgeschichte, Vol. xxxiii (Gütersloh, 1968), pp. 225–343. A good introduction to Müntzer (also regarding the line of questioning pursued here) is still supplied by T. Nipperdey, 'Theologie und Revolution bei Thomas Müntzer', in his *Reformation, Revolution, Utopie: Studien zum 16. Jahrhundert* (Göttingen, 1975), pp. 38–84.

49 D. Martin Luther, *Luthers Werke*, Kritische Ausgabe, Vol. xi (Weimar, 1900), pp. 408–11.

50 E. Wolgast, *Die Wittenberger Theologie und die Politik der evangelischen Stände*, Quellen und Forschungen zur Reformationsgeschichte, Vol. xlvii (Gütersloh, 1977), esp. pp. 20, 26 and 33.

51 A. Laube and H. W. Seiffert (as in n. 6), pp. 203 and 218.

52 G. W. Locher, *Zwinglische Reformation* (as in n. 47), pp. 228–32.

53 Müntzer in a letter addressed to the city of Mühlhausen. Printed in G. Franz (ed.), *Thomas Müntzer* (as in n. 48), p. 473. One must bear in mind that the letter in question was written after Müntzer's interrogation by the nobility.

54 The 'theory of rendering into flesh' belongs, even today, to the seemingly well-established categories for interpreting the relationship between the Reformation and society. The following selected examples are indicative of this tradition in their argumentation: A. Waas (as in n. 22), pp. 74–7. F. Lütge (as in n. 23), pp. 15, 20–21, 29. L. von Muralt, 'Renaissance und Reformation', in *Handbuch der Schweizer Geschichte*, Vol. i (Zürich, 1972), pp. 462–3. P. Baumgart, 'Formen der Volksfrömmigkeit: Krise der alten Kirche und reformatorische Bewegung; zur Ursachenproblematik des "Bauernkrieges"', in P. Blickle (ed.), *Revolte und Revolution in Europa*, Historische Zeitschrift, Beiheft (no. 4, Neue Folge, 1975), p. 204.

55 H. A. Oberman (as in n. 26), 316.

2

Political and Social Norms in Urban Communities in the Holy Roman Empire

HANS-CHRISTOPH RUBLACK

I

To those acquainted with the sources available for the urban history of the German Empire prior to 1800 the issues raised by the following investigation[1] will be familiar, perhaps even usual. It may be precisely this familiarity which explains the seeming disinterest of historical research to concern itself in detail with the social norms integral to urban society. Another reason may be found in the orientation of urban historical research and its preoccupation with legal and social history.[2] Here the task will not be to investigate the fundamental principles which underpin urban society by reverting to an approach which neglects legal and social history and relies solely upon the history of ideas. Such an approach would tend to obscure the true nature of the situation in which these norms were realised. The hypothesis here is that the everyday experience of social action and interaction was above all decisive. This was the formative and as such essentially non-theoretical element.

II

It should be clear that this study in no way claims to be definitive. The illustrations chosen, within the framework of the old German Empire, are taken systematically neither geographically nor chronologically. The urban evidence does suggest a change in social norms around 1500. They become more conscious and tangible and can be expressed in theoretical form while being deliberately applied in conflict situations. Instances are cited unsystematically, from large and small towns alike. This imbalance could be corrected by later studies, but here this can be modified by taking account of the fact that the pre-industrial cities, in comparison to the growing urban centres of the nineteenth century, covered a relatively small area and had a comparatively low population.[3] This ensured that the experience of social contact was personal and concrete and that influences were direct and immediate. Messages were conveyed without secondary symbols or tertiary communication systems. The old European town displayed some aspects of primary groupings. To a lesser extent this is also applicable to the larger towns. Essentially, as Mack Walker has stated, the old European town was in a very real sense a 'home town'[4].

III

The use of the term norm necessitates definition. In this context norms are taken to indicate principles legitimising social action – something which Heinrich Lutz has termed macronorms[5] as opposed to norms which regulate social action: 'Norms are the regulators which effectively determine social behaviour' (R. König).[6]

Social action is thereby held to encompass the entire realm of activities and behaviour which are oriented towards a social system. Yet no fundamental relationship is assumed which might imply that religious activity or legal action, in contrast to the socio-economic determinatives of social action, are secondary or derivative.

IV

Divided into five main sections, this essay is arranged as follows. First there is a description of norms selected non-chronologically. Secondly, and more importantly, instances of the implementation of such norms are cited, that is the way in which these norms were made or became *effective* within the urban context. The third part is concerned with their theoretical rationalisation, followed by a section which raises more general issues, especially the question of the religious legitimation and the flexibility of these norms – essentially the question of whether or not a hierarchical ordering of norms can be detected. The conclusion consists of an outline of certain theoretical implications, particularly ideological problems and the question of 'social control'.

V

The preamble to the 1478 Nuremberg codification of urban law[7] (*Stadtrechtsreformation*) stated that this was designed to advance the common weal:

> 'And as peace, concord and due obedience of the whole community is protected, defended and enacted by an appropriate and fair administering of justice – therefore to the praise of God and to the salutory and blessed increase of the common weal of this honourable city as well as of the entire community' these statutes have been codified.[8]

The same norms recur in the preamble to the Reformation of Worms, dated 1498,[9] although its legal foundation is based on common law, as distinct from Roman law:

> and so justice is a constant mother and ruler of all things, distributing equally and giving to everyone his due, as well as peace and unity without which the common weal cannot endure.[10]

Justice, peace, unity and the common weal are the norms most frequently mentioned. The Nuremberg Reformation places justice before peace, unity and obedience. These concepts are directed towards 'the praise of God' - which can also be formulated as 'God's honour' - and appear to have a co-ordinating function, serving the common weal. The way in which the norms of peace, unity and obedience of the community are brought together is indicative of their function. Norms are envisaged as acting as integrators[11] for the preservation of the legal and political status quo.

A similar classification of norms is discernible in the 'Worms Reformation'. Here too, justice is exalted above all, peace and unity being deemed necessary for the common weal, while obedience is not included. This illustrates the differing formulations and accentuations possible in any catalogue of norms.

At this point we may anticipate an objection. In describing how these norms came to exist and gain validity in the city, it cannot be claimed that they constitute a purely urban phenomenon either in origin or in their development. It is evident that justice, concord and the common weal are universal norms, which just happened to be applied in the urban context. The reference to St Augustine's notion of 'pax et iustitia' as central norms is no less usual than the use of the Thomistic definition, 'Bonum et salus consociatae multitudinis est, ut eius unitas conservetur quae dicitur pax.'[12] The notion of common weal has been thoroughly investigated[13] and it has been shown that the concept is universally applicable. This means, however, that the realisation of this norm may be taken for granted on the grounds of its frequent recurrence. The common weal is contrasted to the individual weal, the latter being more than individual realisation of fortune or personalised struggle for power. Corporations, such as guilds, which deviate from, or act contrary to the system ordained in a town are confronted with the concept of the common weal and compelled to compromise their special interests.[14]

Equally well known was the norm of peace. Implicit in this norm is the specification that 'the peace of law' should be preserved. Thus it was expected

> that all citizens and inhabitants of Frankfurt should swear a common oath, as of old citizens have done, so that all should the better dwell and live with one another in peace, tranquility and greater trust.[15]

This effectively means that the oath which legally constituted the urban corporation was oriented towards peace and unity, the 'pacis unitas'.

Concord as a norm appears for example in the Augsburg chronicles of the fifteenth century which report a fire in the town of Hall in Tirol in 1447. Thus Hector Mülich:[16]

> in holy week the entire city of Hall was burnt out, so that nothing built of wood remained in the whole town. There was a great discord among the citizens, which God punished.

An interesting variation on these events is provided by Burkhard Zink:[17]

> It is said that the citizens of Hall at this time lived together in so unfriendly a fashion and frequently overran one another and had guns and gun-powder in their houses.

Thus the fire was fuelled by household supplies of gunpowder. This prompted Zink to comment:

> Certainly I am of the opinion that this was a penalty and a punishment from God, on account of our great sin, which unfortunately no one will amend.

The difference lies not in that Zink believed any the less that lack of unity among the citizens had incurred the wrath of God, but rather in that the chronicler can view an event which for us would be plausibly explained by a concrete cause, as no less identical with God's punishment; the religious quality of these events is attested by something palpable.[18]

Peace, then, is a concrete norm, which must be placed in a concrete context. This is exemplified in an ordinance from fifteenth-century Strasbourg. A search warrant[19] gives it practical expression in the opening sentence of the city's legislative codex.[20] It states that in Strasbourg 'every person whether he be a stranger or of the city, should enjoy peace at all times.'

Where a criminal act has been committed, any civic authorities present are obliged to enforce peace, apprehend the offenders and resort to legal procedure; that is the well-known peace ordinance (*Friedgebot*). In the absence of civic authorities it becomes the responsibility of each individual citizen to pursue the offenders. Potentially the whole city may be mobilised in this way. The perpetrator of a crime is to be pursued through the streets with hue and cry, a process in which each citizen must participate. Should the offender seek refuge in a house he should be pursued there. In order to prevent him from finding asylum, citizens who at that moment find themselves in churches and monasteries should place themselves before the entrances, effectively blocking the way. The keeper of the cathedral tower should call in all directions 'gerichtio' and sound the main bell three times. At this the gateways should be closed or blocked by the citizens, who should hurry to these points. Even the smaller gateways are to be closed. Traffic on the bridge over the Rhine must be halted and boats forbidden to ferry across. All visitors should return to their lodgings, 'so that no ill befalls them on the streets'. This demonstrates that it was presumed even in a city as large as Strasbourg, that the citizens would recognise an outsider as such, simply because they knew their fellow citizens on sight.

The search and pursuit of a breaker of the peace mobilised the entire city, obliged each citizen to interrupt his work, to restore the state of law for his fellow citizens and to enact the norm of peace, through the act of hue and cry. Peace, law and mutual aid combine in the pursuit of a criminal. In the same way guard duty is exercised as mutual aid, as guaranteed by the norms of peace and concord. This is shown by an address of the Nördlingen council delivered before reading the statute for defence, fire-prevention and guard duty:[21]

> As from the days of our ancestors to this time of ours it has been and still is the proper usage and custom that all those who are citizens or have the right of citizenship, males, young and old, adults who come together once a year, shall bind themselves to one another by their oaths in trust and friendship which they owe by mutual aid and obligation. This is because of concord, peace and tranquillity and in order that we may all live more amicably[22] and more peacefully with one another, since we belong to one another and can thus be of more aid, comfort and assistance and so the more vigorously steadfast against all those who want to oppose us or forget their fidelity. Hence we ward off that which is unjust ... and should pay heed to the following text.

VI

The formulation of the Nuremberg Reformation, that the *aequitas* of the law protects and defends peace and unity, is similar to the terms of the oath, based upon peace and trust, sworn by the citizens of Frankfurt. It is shown to rest upon the medieval legal concept of protection and defence, counsel and aid, and of reciprocity of fidelity. In the oath, however, a particular relationship with the ruling estate is established when the citizen swears obedience to the council by taking his oath.

Before pursuing this line of inquiry we should first classify the socio-political concepts used here. Walter Ullmann[23] has traced two fundamentally different, mutually exclusive, legal and governmental principles in the Middle Ages; the one theocratic and descending, the other populistic and ascending. The latter is founded in the belief that a legally based government is ultimately legitimised by the populace and that purely as a matter of convenience, authority is invested in particular persons for specified periods of time. By contrast, the basic theocratic principle maintains that power is invested in the highest orders, so that all power relationships are derived from above and are legitimised from there.

These concepts are particularly useful and should be tested against our sources. The justification of the theocratic theory is founded on Holy Scripture (Romans 13 and John 19:11: You have no power which does not proceed from on high) and also on medieval theological texts. This political theory of the social body is hierarchically conceived. It has repercussions not only for the legitimation of power but also for the existing order, as Wolfgang Stürner's[24] comments on John of Salisbury (*Policraticus* 1159) and on Thomas Aquinas make clear. The theocratic line of thought leads to the construction of a hierarchy in which power is devolved through different levels. Hence within this organic image the servants of God, the clergy, assume the position of the soul, the head represents the princes and the feet, which support the body, the peasants and artisans. The most important task of the upper level of the hierarchy is to realise and to recognise the *aequitas* of God. Even though the *salus publica* is given shape throughout the different levels of this hierarchy, the interpretation of the actual meaning of justice and common weal is the prerogative of those endowed with *ratio*, that is the princes.

Thomas Aquinas in *De regno sive de regimine principum ad regem Cypri*[25] (1260–5) likewise views the *respublica* as analogous to the body. He places the leading power above the multitude of individuals, who must be directed in the pursuit of the *proprium bonum*, which can be guaranteed only by the knowledge of the *bonum commune*. Here the concept of the common weal is to be interpreted from above. The canonists also assign a protective function in the community to the clergy and the ruling authorities:

> Sed ius publicum dicitur quod pertinet (ad) rem publicam; et sic non a populo sed a re publica dicitur publicum. Hoc autem est, quod est de prerogativa imperatoris et sacerdotum et aliorum, quorum precipue est tueri enim rempublicam et ei providere in sacris ... et sacerdotibus et magistratibus (Sum *Antiquitate et tempore* relating to dist. 1, can. 11).[26]

The theocratic interpretation allocates norms at the top of the hierarchy. The essential duty of a king is to maintain *pax et iustitia. Iustitia* is instrumental to the preservation of peace. *Utilitas publica*, according to Ullmann,[27] is derived from the concept of protection. According to this interpretation, the population was to be taught rather than followed (*docendus non sequendus*). If the population did not comply they were designated as a 'rabble', a widely held medieval and post-medieval notion[28] which regarded the *tumultuositas* of the people as constantly 'prone to insanity'.

How did life in town and village communities accord with this theoretical framework? We need only recall that in the cities the oath served as a constitutive element, ensuring the peace of law, upon which was based the protection in law, defence and mutual aid of those bound by the oath. This theory of ascendance was experienced in the cities as 'a natural product of living together'.[29] The oath, taken on a specific day (*Schwörtag*), made manifest the unity of the citizens and gave concrete expression to the *pacis unitas*. Equally mundane and non-theoretical were the social activities involved in guard duty, church services, council and community gatherings.

In addition to the horizontal dimension of an oath sworn by equal citizens a vertical element was introduced through the pledge of faithfulness and obedience sworn to the council, as in Cologne in 1355:[30]

> First of all they should swear to be faithful and subject to the council and city of Cologne;

and in Schlettstadt:[31]

> One should swear to the mayor and council, equally to every guildmaster, to be obedient unto them.

In the final years of the Holy Roman Empire Johann Jakob Moser defined this relationship as follows:

> The citizens and other inhabitants of an imperial city have a collective and individual duty vis-à-vis their authorities, similar to the allegiance owed by subjects to the territorial rulers of the Empire, which, firstly, consists of paying them honour and, secondly, of rendering them obedience.[32]

This definition is connected to the vertical dimension. It has a levelling effect on the citizens and those merely resident within the city. There is an element of tension in the differentiation made between the latter and territorial subjects, because citizens of imperial cities are seen as 'subordinates but not subjects' (*Untergebene seynd sie, aber keine Untertanen*). Moser points to the inherent tension between the two elements of the medieval oath: the promises of allegiance and obedience. He shows that the promise of obedience could assume greater importance than that of allegiance.

The fundamental legal significance of the urban oath has been described by Ebel,[33] who points out that the city as a whole was permeated with oaths. Moser already attributed the yearly swearing of the citizen's oath to the annual change in government and referred to the southern German cities of Regensburg, Überlingen and Esslingen[34] as examples. Ebel[35] also confirmed that this tradition tended to filter out towards the north of Germany.

Before Ebel, the numerous oaths of city officials had already been commented on pointedly by Hans Fehr:[36] 'The divisive forces inherent in the masses have to be checked by the oath. Urban oaths were a juridical or legal counterweight to social mistrust. They established a legal bond which one could not otherwise have expected of the urban ideal.' Fehr added more provocatively: 'The history of the city ... [is] a history of artful betrayals', which oaths were to counteract.

This would appear to be somewhat misleading, though any historian would take seriously the reference to individual benefit and social differentiation contained therein. The prevailing explanation of the multiplicity of civic oaths concentrates on locating the origin of the urban oath in the guilds. As Oexle has demonstrated,[37] we find in the guilds the necessary elements which later characterise the *conjurationes* of the commune. They were: the parity of members (horizontal dimension), peace and the union (protective function), the universality of the *fait social total*, the brotherhood which made an everyday obligation of these elements. It is the norm of the *fraterna dilectio*, essential to the guild, which seems to distinguish its oath-taking ceremony from the urban *conjuratio*. In the urban context this norm can be encountered only rarely. The fact that this norm of brotherly love could be referred to as late as the sixteenth century will be discussed later.

If one views the guilds as associations which represented an early model of the urban community and where peace formed a constitutive element, then it is clear that the movement for the peace of God which conveyed the norm of peace to the citizens through the medium of the urban leagues, reinforced the norm's legitimation by connecting it to pre-existing concepts. So the alliance between Mainz and Worms of 1254[38] referred to established practice, when it deduced the basic norms of peace and unity from theological notions: 'Mirifici creatoris clementia pacem et concordiam in hominibus operatur.'

In the sixteenth century religious conviction could in fact run contrary to the urban norms instead of strengthening them. So the Anabaptists could not be integrated into the community, since they refused to take the oath.[39] This rather was a result of, than something directly caused by, their heterodoxy. By indicating their refusal they *ipso facto* excluded themselves from the city just as effectively as if they had committed perjury.

Less well known is that in 1526 a Nuremberg resident petitioned the preachers to take a stand against the increasing number of oaths.[40] This petition supports Fehr's statement quoted above. The unknown author objects to the 'ungodly and shameful misuse of the daily swearing of oaths'. He argues that

> the swearing of oaths [occurs] in this praiseworthy city unfortunately more often than probably in any other place, far and wide, clearly stemming from an old, evil and unfounded misuse [and it is] also employed in entirely minor matters which at times relate to nothing more than a hazel nut, so daily and over generalities ... that far too many swear, who know little or are hardly aware of what they are swearing.

The taking of an oath once was deemed sufficient by the unknown author. Honour was to be trusted, the frequent swearing was a 'deprecation, as if one party no longer placed trust in the other'.

This suggestion was not taken up. It seems that such a strict biblicism could not be adopted even in those urban communities where preaching had to be based on the *sola scriptura* principle. The petition reveals, however, that the Reformation released energy which tended to disrupt the traditional socio-political concept of order.

Another development in Reformation teaching, which contradicted the social order of the medieval town, as far as it was conceived horizontally, was the dissolution of the confraternities. As Oexle has recently shown,[41] Luther had little or no understanding of the brotherhoods, as a result of his theological reassessment of good works. For this reason the urban Reformation city allowed these socio-religious institutions to fall by the wayside.

VII

The value of conflict analysis for the better understanding of the functioning of constitutions was mentioned by Aristotle in his *Politics*:[42]

> it is clear that we can get to know how constitutions are preserved if we know how they break down. For opposites effect opposites, and decline is in opposition to preservation.

The way in which norms were put to use shall be investigated here based on two cases of conflict in southern German cities, one from fifteenth-century Augsburg, the other from Nördlingen at the time of the Peasants' War.

The first is well known. It is the case of Ulrich Schwarz.[43] Hektor Mülich reports what in his eyes amounted to a spectacular scandal.[44]

> On the 18th day of April [1478] Ulrich Schwarz, mayor at that time, was hanged. And he had been mayor for four consecutive years and was more powerful than anyone had ever been in Augsburg. And he was a carpenter's son and was

> the salt merchants' guildmaster and whatever he willed was to be done.

The case was so unusual that Jos Ohnsorg, a fellow mayor in office, collapsed in the street 'and died a sudden death, from which God preserve us'[45].

Schwarz, who had risen from the quarters of the poor, was responsible for the execution of Hans Vittel. As an envoy of the Augsburg council, this patrician councillor allegedly had let it be known at the Emperor's court that the affairs of the Augsburg council had fallen into disorder, because illegal activities had to be kept secret. The emperor learned that a guild master finally had to be executed, because he had covered up a robbery. Schwarz had apparently dispatched his son-in-law, the city's syndic, to accompany Vittel to the imperial court. But further charges could not be produced against Vittel, the council's envoy, for the Emperor had retreated with him. Confronted with these accusations, Vittel refused to take an exculpatory oath. Schwarz acted hastily, secured Vittel's conviction and denied him mercy, even though Vittel's daughter called upon six hundred pregnant women to pray for her father. Walking up to the execution block Vittel could cast political considerations to the winds and publicly accused Schwarz of being a thief: he had robbed the council against God's will and in violation of honour and justice.

The execution of Schwarz in 1478 was a result of imperial intervention. A later and partisan source[46] concerning these proceedings presents the overthrow of the mayor as follows:

> So that an honourable council may be purged and purified through a legal process from such disobedient and disreputable people.

The indictment of Schwarz is a compact document for our investigation of urban norms. It accused Schwarz of having acted in his office contrary to the common weal and of having sought his individual benefit; he had violated honour and trust and broken his oath, especially in acting as mediator in marital conflicts and in taking money or items of value for this. He has misappropriated public funds, as well as the wealth of the Hospital of the Holy Spirit; as the text pithily put it: 'And betrayed the Holy Ghost of his possession'.[47] Finally, as in Vittel's case, he had allowed respectable citizens to be spied upon and had fabricated reports to bring them into disrepute and damage their life, honour and goods. Schwarz thus was cited for corruption as well as abuse of office, and as an offender against honour, law and the common weal.

Attempts by historians to correct these accusations against Schwarz which were put in terms of aristocratic parties, repeatedly proved abortive, since the archival documents in question have apparently been destroyed.[48] So Schwarz' indictment may, in fact, be misleading. It demonstrates, however, the way in which norms were used politically in the city. To make this perfectly clear I present a synopsis given by Phillippe Dollinger,[49] who listed the allegations which the rebellious citizens of the fourteenth century raised against the patricians:

- Abuse of power
- Outrage against fellow citizens
- Partisanship in the administration of justice
- Arrogance
- Corrupt handling of finance
- Secrecy concerning the use of public funds

The charges are readily transferrable into the corresponding norms of law, peace and common weal.

A century later the same norms were invoked in complaints against the populist mayor Schwarz. This has a twofold significance: first, that the norms had remained constant, and secondly, that they had been brought into play by parties in conflict with each other.

During the Peasants' War the Nördlingen council allowed speeches[50] to be composed which were directed either at the large council or at the community as a whole. The council feared that some citizens who sympathised with the peasants assembling some 5 km east of the city near Deiningen[51] might co-operate with the insurgents. From spring into autumn 1525 there was a series of such addresses, all of which made use of norms in appealing to the citizens. One of the earliest, addressed to the large council, dated 28 March 1525, stated:

> Even those with the least understanding appreciate that no empire, principality, territory or city can endure without peaceful unity. The weak and small are raised through peace and unity, the great decay through lack of peace.[52]

This traditional theme appears frequently in the urban tradition around 1500, as for example in a tract written by the Nuremberg town clerk, Lazarus Spengler, entitled *An Admonition and Instruction to Virtuous Behaviour* (*c.* 1509–10):[53]

> Then what is there more devilish, importunate and damaging than opposition, trouble and disunity over against that which is lovelier, more true and beneficial, as are peace and unity. As we see through daily experience peace and harmony can raise little things and cause them to develop. But large things, an entire community and government can come to nought and completely pass away through disunity and lack of peace.[54]

By this allusion to experience Spengler obscures the fact that this tradition extends back not only to the Golden Bull[55] but also to Matthew 12:25 and Sallust's *Jugurtha*.

More than four years after the Peasants' War the Nördlingen town clerk, Georg Mair, indicated that Christ had said in his Holy Gospel: every realm which is divided against itself will fall down. But through the peace of God and unity, Mair continued his comment on Matthew 12:25,[56] an empire shall be increased, just as the pagan Sallust[57] has shown: with good judgement and fortuitous unity a small empire can develop, but then through devilish dissension and discord great empires can collapse and go to waste. The town clerk also added that all laws should strive for peace and unity.

This appeal was pronounced in 1529 – at a time when the Nördlingen council had to decide whether to adhere to the Protestation of Speyer or to declare its obedience to the emperor.[58] The council chose the latter, on the basis of biblical and other sanctions of peace and unity.

Another issue related to this theme was discussed in Nördlingen in 1525, where a demonstration of sympathy with the peasants could mean the city's actual defection from the empire, as well as a potential alienation from the Swabian League. The councillor's speeches were designed to bring the citizens to support the council's policy of preventing such co-operation with the peasants. To this end, the basic norms were put to use. In other speeches, however, the aforementioned norms appear to be underplayed. At the beginning of May, a speech invoked in detail the tradition of the imperial city.[59] It depicted the way in which Nördlingen had been transferred to the empire from the overlordship of St Emmeran of Regensburg, thereby gaining imperial privileges. It was held, however, that the citizens had been instrumental in making the city what it was. Following the city fire in 1238 it was the citizens themselves who had rebuilt the town. The walling-in of the city between 1327 and the fifteenth century was likewise a product of their collective labour. Religious motivation recedes into the background: unity is legitimised by tradition and freedom, according to another speech, seen as a thing of incalculable value. Essentially, what was stressed was the city's autonomy.

These speeches, with their changing mixture and accentuation of norms, were to produce the same effect. The community should not side with the peasants but follow the council's policy of alliance with the Swabian League. To achieve this, norms were invoked in a highly flexible manner.

The conscious aim underlying the reference to these norms is verified by a document[60] from the consultations of the large council, dated 28 March, outlining the catch-phrases which served to elaborate the speech to the community. Here one reads 'Above all things brotherly love should be called upon';[61] again it is noted 'Do not forget brotherly love'.[62]

The catch-phrase 'brotherly love', sometimes also coined as 'dear brethren', occurs frequently in sources which originated among the rebellious peasants.[63] Leonhard von Eck, the Bavarian counsellor, commented sarcastically that he rather wished to share with the Fuggers as well, and thus saw it as nothing other that an attack on wealth.[64] The Nördlingen council could proclaim the catch-phrase as a norm, which had a long tradition within the city and was one they used consciously. Additional strength was brought to the relationship between those who had sworn the oath, by *mutua caritas* (mutal aid). *Muta caritas* was, of course, a highly sanctioned religious norm.

The result of our two case studies may be summarised as follows:

(1) Norms were validated in a conscious way.
(2) Norms could, as in Nördlingen, be arranged in different ways, as well as be substituted for each other and interchanged.

VIII

If, in the city, norms were first and foremost a matter of political, legal and social convention inherent in everyday life, it should not be assumed that a theory of norms developed in the city which was founded upon a hierarchical ordering of norms, such as that proposed by learned theologians in the Middle Ages.

One can, at any rate, determine that explicit reference to norms in urban sources increases around 1500 – the preambles to the 'Reformations' of urban law bear witness to this, as do the previously discussed Nördlingen addresses. Heinrich Lutz has ascertained that the period of the Renaissance and Humanism was characterised by 'the reflection of, and a decisive wish to employ, the Christian norms in this world'.[65] This essentially corresponds with our observations without necessitating further elaboration of the relationship between the city and humanism.

Before considering the rationalisation of norms, I should like to exemplify the non-theoretical attitude towards norms. The description by the Nuremberg patrician, Christoph Scheurl, of the Nuremberg constitution, which he claimed to have written in only ten hours, is a case in point. Scheurl was a member of the association which had formed around Johannes Staupitz, Provincial of the Observant Augustinians, to whom the description was addressed.[66]

> In beginning my project I should first point out that the Nuremberg people share the assumption that all wisdom, counsel and regime is to be sought and desired alone from and through God.

Following such an opening one would expect a theological-political tract to follow. But Scheurl continues:

> It is a commonplace, known by everyone, that if a man intends to undertake something, it is God who directs him.

Scheurl's informing his readers of such a commonplace, in treating the religious dimension of the urban community, is of greater importance since in 1517 Scheurl translated into German Staupitz' tract *Libellus de exsecutione aeternae prae-*

destinationis,[67] and thus refers to the deeper theological dimensions of the saying he quotes.

> And it must also be taken as true, that the instability of nature has no stable working and the transitoriness of nature no staying power. Thus shield yourself that you do not eternalise any human work and be wary that alone from God proceedeth any constancy.[68]

Scheurl certainly knew that this commonplace was a quotation from Proverbs 16:9: 'A man's heart desireth his way, but the Lord directeth his steps.'[69] But he pretended that the notion expressed by this commonplace was derived from everyday life. Without theological digression he thus considered communal practice: when decisions are to be taken on important issues, the council shall call upon the priests to pray and to organise a procession. He thereby points to the custom of celebrating a Mass of the Holy Spirit before the councillors are nominated:

> Therewith the common folk were exhorted to pray, to call upon God in unison, so that God might extend his blessing ensuring that such people would rule, who are endowed with wisdom and understanding and also have the fear of God, so that the civic offices would be given to fervent God-fearing men, rather than those men being assigned to offices they personally desired.[70]

This demonstrates Scheurl's disregard of theological reasoning. It suggests an attitude of practical Christianity, that is an understatement, similar to that used by the seventeenth-century Hamburg mayor, Vincent Möller, when he dismissed the question of the citizens' committees, 'whether the status of this republic is of an aristocratic or democratic nature' ('an sit aristocraticus an sit democraticus'), as useless scholastic tittle-tattle – a dismissal not lacking political intent.[71] Scheurl, however, in this case diverging from Möller's pragmatic style, which may have been his own as well, handled the question of 'an sit aristocraticus an sit democraticus' with clarity and by emphasising its theological underpinning.[72]

The Nuremberg council was recruited among the patricians whose ancestors had sat in government. The 'common folk' have 'no power', Scheurl argued,

> it does not belong to their estate, since all power comes from God and good government belongs only to those who have been endowed with special wisdom by the creator of all things and nature.

It is clear that this theological legitimation of patrician government far exceeds the terms of Romans 13, a text which was used already at the end of the Middle Ages to justify the position of urban governments.[73] Scheurl made a very hidden reference to the virtue of nobility as wisdom.[74] Equally unconvincing for some citizens may have been his allusion to the natural order of God's creation. But here, too, Scheurl's theological theorising ends rather abruptly. He thus presents himself as one who describes political practice non-theoretically.

At the same time, in 1501, a theory of the city drawing on norms is furnished by Jacob Wimpheling in the second book of his *Germania*.[75] Wimpheling called himself 'Germaniae membrum et imperialis oppidi filius' (a German and son of an imperial city).[76] Concord and unity are viewed by him not so much as fortresses against an external threat, but rather as a buffer against partisanship and dissension within the city. In underlining this norm with the catch-phrase *mutua caritas*, he brings to mind the tradition of the *fraterna dilectio* and mutual aid. Concord, so Wimpheling continues, is aligned to the common weal.[77] Common weal is the equivalent of the Latin *respublica*.[78] Discord arose, according to the humanist, from social differentiation. A long paragraph[79] analyses how the three estates – ecclesiastical, noble and artisan – are represented in the organic image as eyes, heart and hands and how they are interrelated. It is only the love of the common weal which can dam up the springs of inner dissension. The doctrine of the three estates, superimposed upon the complex urban social structure, looks somewhat strained. It thus relates a blurred image of social reality and proves to be alien to the urban confederacy. The distance between social reality and this interpretation, which relies upon the doctrine of the three estates, indicates that Wimpheling's rationalising theory was not gained inductively from urban practice, but rather constitutes a detached view, which James M. Kittelson termed a 'myth of civic spirituality'.[80]

Social harmony places the regime under the title of law:

> ne potentiores humilem, ne opulenti egenum, ne proceres plebem ullo pactu non solum non opprimere, sed aspernari et despicere conentur et ne ullus status alium labefactare aut diminuere quaeret.[81]

Peace, concord, *respublica*, as the common weal, guarantee harmony.

> The ideal is a society free of conflict in which each estate is assigned a specific position and has a definite task to perform and therewith at once automatically works to the benefit of the whole. So, the meaning of its task should be made clear to each individual estate. That is the surest way to avert struggles for a more favourable position in the social hierarchy.

In these words Winfried Schulze[82] characterises the function of this theory, as it appears in pamphlets relating to the Turks of *c.*1600.

The application of this model of harmony to the history of the Middle Ages is comparable to the present-day understanding of the late medieval and early modern city as based upon consensus.[83] Integrative norms, as used in the urban context, and the theory of the city as interpreted by Wimpheling, the *imperialis oppidi filius*, show that this modern interpretation can be verified historically. The above quotation from Wimpheling shows precisely that the reality of the old European city is only partially covered by this interpretation, and that it is necessary to question this interpretation in terms of the doctrine of the estates. With his postulate of harmony Wimpheling obscures the nature of this truly dichotomic structure,[84] which he himself describes by contrasting *potens – humilis, opulens – egenus*, and *proceres – plebs*. This raises the question of the ideological character of norms, a theme which will be taken up in the final section of this paper.

IX

Next, certain problem areas should be discussed.

(1) 'There is nothing more axiomatic for medieval thought than that all law is founded in God.'[85] 'Axiomatic' means that the religious legitimation of norms may be implied even where it is not specifically referred to. 'Where peace is, there is God himself', declares a police ordinance from early-sixteenth-century Constance.[86] The thirteenth-century tradition of the territorial leagues for the maintenance of peace in the treaties of which Christ appears as *auctor pacis*,[87] has already been mentioned.

For Wimpheling likewise the common weal has a religious foundation:[88]

> For any good, the more general it is, so much is it holier, so much is it also godlier. For in whom true love is, to them will be conferred a firm trust in the common weal.[89]

The Nuremberg Reformation depicts the increase of the common weal as salvatory and blessed.

That concord is protected by God and enacted by sanctions against discord is made clear by the Augsburg chroniclers, with reference to the example of the city of Hall. Also the obedience of the community to the urban authorities was religiously legitimised as in Nördlingen in 1480:[90]

> As we find in Holy Scriptures, that all authority descends from God, the Lord . . . so we can understand that whosoever will be elected to be in power should use this power correctly, since it comes from God, that all the subjects should be obedient to those placed over them, as they have the care and must account for what they do, so that they can do this with joy and without sighs, which is their benefit.

In all this the election to office is upheld. But the highest authority belongs to those in possession of power coming directly from God. And the nature of their activity is perceived as 'descending': they must take care of and be accountable for the conduct of their subjects. The Augsburg town clerk, Hans Trumer, in 1601 put it succinctly:[91] 'The authorities are made in God's image, as power proceeds from God.'

Within this paternalistic definition of the function of government, the obligation to maintain social welfare could also be invoked. In Nuremberg in March 1525, Osiander preached on the doctrine of the two-realms.[92] Immediately printed and distributed throughout the city's unruly territory by the Nuremberg council, this sermon spoke of the duty to care for social welfare. 'The government should not rule just for itself, but also for all its subjects' benefit.' Naturally, Osiander upheld the commandment of obedience to the government and defended the suppression of revolts, 'so that peace and concord, as much as is ever possible, will be retained'.

The tendency towards a paternalistic explanation runs contrary to Martin Bucer's tract of 1523, entitled *That one should not live for himself but for others.*[93] Bucer laid particular emphasis on the 'service to the whole community, to achieve their welfare by the preservation of general peace and equity'.[94] The interpretation developed in this tract partially relies on Aristotle. The distinction between a good prince and a tyrant is taken from Erasmus' *Institutio principis christiani*,[95] expressed in Bucer's version as 'the prince solely serves the welfare of his subjects, the tyrant is self-seeking',[96] and in the Erasmian formulation as 'Id vt compedio dicam, hac nota principem a tyranno distinguit in politicis Aristoteles, quod hic suis studet commodis, ille reipublicae'.[97] Herding indicates this in his commentary on *Policraticus* of John of Salisbury, which, first printed in 1476 and reprinted in 1513 in Paris, might have been used by Erasmus. The differentiation between *politias rectas* and *vitiosas* had already been worked out by Thomas Aquinas, whose commentary on the *Politics* of Aristotle apparently was not readily available to Bucer.

Thus, there is no doubt that basic norms were religiously legitimised. But this raises the question, as yet unanswered, of how to define this relationship with some precision and how to arrange the constellations and to place the accentuations. It would be more precise to ascertain which traditions of theological and political theory, which political theologies favoured specific accents, and which situations and which social and political constellations defined or gave way to an explicit legitimation.

(2) In the texts discussed here norms are continuously referred to in relation to one another. Peace is law, the honour of the city is its law,[98] the honour of the city and the honour of God can be identified with one another,[99] law and justice are cited as the foundation of peace and unity, and honour and the common weal are seen as identical, as in an early decree of the Nuremberg council: 'Only that which is done with honour, would be beneficial to the town and community.'[100]

'The object of law is the common good', according to Zasius's formulation;[101] 'it effects a salvatory unity.' Hans Sachs's attempt[102] to present the self-seeking Hans Widerporst as an egoist is instructive in this respect:

> From this every man should note/if he wants to have peace and tranquillity/he should avoid acting contrarily/and not resort to opposition.[103]

In living up to this ideal of the common weal, Sachs even recommends the toleration of suffering:

> Suffer as much as any man has suffered/these are the ways to peace and unity.[104]

The norms appear here fused into a pattern and detached from any hierarchical order. They are, then, interchangeable and at least functionally equivalent, as those mentioned in the addresses to the Nördlingen council discussed above. This does not impair their validity, as they are all equally founded on religion. The question is raised whether the equivalence of norms can result from their common religious foundation. This would render their use more flexible and permit their substitution for each other.

(3) On the other hand, the concreteness of medieval thought facilitates the specification of norms. This is most palpable in regard to norms functioning as 'regulative ideas', that is norms which have no specific contents, such as the common weal. It can be applied to the urban exchequer,[105] but also to works of public defence and public buildings. The Worms Reformation encouraged endowment by wills:[106]

> What could more be wanted than to further the common weal and to give something, especially here in our city of Worms, to build and maintain in the same our city's walls, gateways, towers, ditches, fortresses, bridges, ways and steps ... Thereby all inhabitants of the city [can live] in liberty, for there is nothing more noble on earth than the maintenance of peace and security.

Likewise the recommendation of the Nuremberg clergy and

jurists concerning the right of citizenship of the clergy, of 8 May 1525,[107] stated:

> The clergy must bear the same taxes as the citizens, and above all [contribute to the maintenance of] that which relates to the common weal, such as bridges, ways, steps, dams to protect against the waters, the towers, ditches, barbicans, walls and artillery houses of the entire city and finally bear all the burdens of the common weal.

Here the norms are tied to things which are more concrete, the 'moral economy'[108] is considered in that which is tangible. This raises the question of how legitimising norms can be separated other than analytically from regulating norms. Or – to express this in the categories formulated by Heinrich Lutz – the non-theoretical and concrete use of norms in the city makes it doubtful whether the distinction between the level of macronorms and that of micronorms can be upheld.

X

The above observation rather favours a theoretical approach[109] which I would like to make explicit in conclusion. It arises from the assumption that cultural symbols such as norms not only materialise, but also originate in social action, though in the face of given theological presuppositions, this approach seems too abstract to the historian of the medieval or early modern city. At least these symbols appear as everyday norms in everyday social action and as such are perpetuated without being rationalised. Daily interaction replaced the theory, because the concerns of daily life are essentially pre-theoretical.

This is all the more so, because, according to an elementary assumption in the socio-ecological theory[110] – reverted here – the shorter the social distance, the smaller and more compact is the settlement and the greater the division of labour and internal differentiation, so much greater is the need for integration.

XI

The observation that everyday norms could be formulated both explicitly and theoretically raises the question of the ideological nature of urban norms. 'Ideology' is here understood only as narrowly circumscribed, abstract norms expressing interests on the level of the idea. The Nördlingen evidence from the period of the Peasants' War (cited above), illustrates the conscious, politically motivated invocation of norms in an attempt to secure the regime by establishing a communal consensus. This included the proclamation of 'verbal norms', usually called 'integrative norms', which apparently were met with general acceptance and were considered as valid and fundamental. The party proclaiming them did not actually oppose a different set of norms. In fact, there was no discussion about norms as such.

Likewise the norms appear as genuinely held to those who proclaim them in order to assure their validity. Norms are not invoked, therefore, if there is no belief in their reality. This explains why they could be used as integrative norms, that is as norms designed to secure law and order. Norms could be put to use in order to ensure a communal consensus in favour of the authorities. But norms were not just manipulated; they were invoked in accordance with their specific purposes. Under these circumstances they were held as valid. The authorities did not make the people believe that which they themselves did not believe. But, as always, once a norm was proclaimed it was interpreted by the government. This interpretative process relied on the ideological use of a norm. It could be used to ensure the interests of those in power. Concrete norms could, of course, also be interpreted in the perspective of differing interests. The invocation of norms in conflicts indicates that the fundamental norms as such were not considered controversial, rather that the interests of the parties involved were transferred to the level of norms.

XII

In another context norms had a function in the system of social control[111] of the city as well as of the Holy Roman Empire. Here also, their manipulation in an attempt to maintain conformity was but one possible means of ensuring stability – a process which has not yet been sufficiently substantiated. The examination of norms, and of the experience which rendered them valid in the context of the functions of social conrol, raises the question whether there were other institutions in which norms were ingrained. To this the interaction model endeavours to give a partial answer: the activities of the urban community were continuously related to norms. But this observation relates only to a symbolic level of the organisation of social control, not to the physiomaterial level.

The question as to how public norms and those of primary social groupings, such as the family and the house, were brought to harmony must remain open. Congruence can be suggested for 'peace' and 'concord'.[112] This has yet to be proved in greater detail. There are differences in this repect regarding the notion of common weal because it opposes personal benefit which is not tied to public welfare.[113] Therewith we have to deal with a rivalry on the organisational level of social control. This was all the more so in cases where the city was structured, or rather stratified, by division of labour. Division of labour within the community produced rivalries which were clearly apparent among the guilds – tensions which through greater pressure of conformity and institutional integrative regulators had to be controlled and checked. To put it more simply: social mobility and differentiation worked against integration. It is no accident, therefore, that integrative norms gain expression when social systems are threatened by disintegration, that is, when conflict arises.

The model of the urban community based on harmony and consensus - however much the cities of the Holy Roman Empire could present themselves in this fashion - covers and obscures tensions and conflicts which were a constitutive element of urban social action, as well as of the development of norms and their function.

Notes: Chapter 2

1 This paper was originally read to the seminar of the Institut für Vergleichende Städteforschung in Münster. It has profited from the discussions held in Münster and in the seminar of the German Historical Institute, London, as well as from critical assessment by the team of Z 2, SFB 8, at the University of Tübingen. Special thanks for their comments must go to Erdmann Weyrauch, Thomas A. Brady, Berndt Hamm and Christoph Burger.

2 This has recently been observed by M. Brecht, 'Luthertum als politische und soziale Kraft in den Städten', in F. Petri (ed.), *Kirche und gesellschaftlicher Wandel in deutschen und niederländischen Städten der werdenden Neuzeit*, Städteforschung, Reihe A, Vol. x (Cologne and Vienna, 1980), pp. 1-21. See also H.-C. Rublack, 'Probleme der Sozialtopographie im Mittelalter und in der frühen Neuzeit', in W. Ehbrecht (ed.), *Voraussetzungen und Methoden geschichtlicher Städteforschung*, Städteforschung, Reihe A, Vol. vii (Cologne and Vienna, 1979), p. 177, n. 2. A bias in favour of urban history of the Middle Ages can also be detected in the distribution of courses taught in history departments of West German universities. In the summer term of 1980, 60 per cent of the urban history courses offered covered the medieval period, 11 per cent the nineteenth and twentieth centuries, and only 7 per cent the early modern period. See *Archiv für Kommunalwissenschaft*, xix (1980), 353 ff.

3 H. Stoob, 'Stadtformen und städtisches Leben im späten Mittelalter', in Stoob (ed.), *Die Stadt: Gestalt und Wandel bis zum industriellen Zeitalter* Vol. i (Cologne and Vienna, 1979), pp. 157-94.

4 M. Walker, *German Home Towns: Community, State and General Estate, 1648-1871* (Ithaca, NY and London, 1971).

5 H. Lutz, 'Normen und gesellschaftlicher Wandel zwischen Renaissance und Revolution - Differenzierung und Säkularisierung', *Saeculum*, xxvi (1975), 166-80. 'Macronorms' can also be termed 'values'.

6 R. König, 'Soziale Normen', in W. Bernsdorf (ed.), *Wörterbuch der Soziologie*, 3 vols, Fischer tb, no. 6133, Vol. iii (Frankfurt/Main, 1972), p. 734.

7 W. Kunkel (ed.), *Quellen zur Neueren Privatrechtsgeschichte Deutschlands*, Vol. i/l: Ältere Stadtrechtsreformationen (Weimar, 1936), pp. 1 ff.

8 ibid., p. 3: 'Und nach dem auch in zimlicher und geleicher austailung der gerechtikait nit allain geschützt, beschirmt und gehanthabt würdet fride, eynigkait und zymliche gehorsame der ganzen gemainde ... hierumb got zu lobe und zu hailsamer und seliger merung gemaines nutzes diser erbern stat und auch der ganzen gemainde.'

9 ibid., pp. 96 ff.

10 ibid., p. 97: 'Und aber die gerechtikeit ein stanthaftige muter, der ding aller regirerin und glymesserin, einem yedem gibt das syn, auch frid und einikeit one die der gemeine nütz nit bestehen mag.'

11 W. Bernsdorf, 'Integration, soziale', in *Wörterbuch der Soziologie* (as in n. 6), Vol. ii, pp. 373–7.

12 W. Janssen, 'Friede', in O. Brunner *et al.* (eds) *Geschichtliche Grundbegriffe*, (Stuttgart, 1975), Vol. ii, p. 552.

13 W. Merck, 'Der Gedanke des gemeinen Besten in der deutschen Staats- und Rechtsentwicklung', in *Festschrift Alfred Schulze* (Weimar, 1934), pp. 451–520. More specialised is E.-W. Kohls, *Die Schule bei Martin Bucer in ihrem Verhältnis zu Kirche und Obrigkeit*, Pädagogische Forschungen, Vol. xxii (Heidelberg, 1963), pp. 121–9. See also B. Eckert, 'Der Gedanke des Gemainen Nutzen in der Staatslehre des Johannes Ferrarius', *Jahrbuch der hessischen kirchengeschichtlichen Vereinigung*, xxvii (1976), 157–209.

14 For Wimpheling, see T. A. Brady, jun., 'The themes of social structure, social conflict and civic harmony in Jacob Wimpheling's "Germania"', *Sixteenth Century Journal*, iii (2, 1972), 65–76, esp. 74. Analagous the 'ius publicum' and 'ius privatum': W. Mager, *Zur Entstehung des modernen Staatsbegriffs*, Abhandlungen der Akademie der Wissenschaften und Literatur, geistes- und sozialwiss. Klasse, 1968, no. 9 (Wiesbaden, 1968), p. 408.

15 F. Keutgen (ed.), *Urkunden zur Städtischen Verfassungsgeschichte*, (Berlin, 1901; repr. Aalen, 1965), p. 247: 'Das alle burgere und inwonere zu Frankenfurt glichlich einen gemeynen eid tun und sweren sollen als man von alder die burger enphangen hat, uf das wir alle debas in fridde und gemach deste getrulicher by ein bliben und gesiczen mogen.'

16 'Chronik des Hector Mülich', in F. Roth (ed.), *Die Chroniken der schwäbischen Städte: Augsburg*, Vol. iii (=*Die Chroniken der deutschen Städte*, Vol. xxii), 2nd edn (Göttingen, 1965), p. 88.

17 'Die Chronik des Burkard Zink, 1386–1468', in C. Hegel (ed.), *Die Chroniken der deutschen Städte: Augsburg*, Vol. v, 2nd edn (Göttingen, 1965), pp. 182–3. K. Schnath, *Die Augsburger Chronik des Burkhard Zink: Eine Untersuchung zur reichsstädtischen Geschichtsschreibung*, phil. diss. (Munich, 1958). E. Maschke, 'Der wirtschaftliche Aufstieg des Burkhard Zink (geb. 1396, gest. 1474/5 in Augsburg', in O. Brunner (ed.), *Festschrift Hermann Aubin zum 80. Geburtstag*, Vol. i (Wiesbaden, 1965), pp. 235–62.

18 L. Graf zu Dohna, *Reformatio Sigismundi: Beiträge zum Verständnis einer Reformschrift des 15. Jahrhunderts*, Veröffentlichungen des Max-Planck-Instituts für Geschichte, Vol. iv (Göttingen, 1960), p. 23.

19 J. Bruckner, *Strassburger Zunft- und Polizeiverordnungen des 14. und 15. Jahrhunderts* (Strassburg, 1889), pp. 23–30.

20 ibid., p. 23.

21 'Alß dann von vnnser Eltfordern bis her vntz vff vnns gepflegen vnnd gewonhait gewesen vnd noch ist, das alle die, So alhie Burger sind oder Burgerrecht haben, mans namen Jung vnd alt, die Zu Iren tagen komen sind, des Jars ainest Zuainanderkomen vnnd sich sollher trw vnd fruntschaft, So sy mit bystand ain annder schuldig vnnd pflichtig sind, mit Irn aiden Zu ainander verpunden söllen, als Ir dann Itzo alle darumb byainander sind, Darumb durch ainigkait, frids vnd gemachs vnnd auch vmb des willen, das wir alle dest früntlicher vnd fridlicher byainander sitzen als wir Zuainander gehörn vnd ain annder des hilflicher, trostlicher vnd bygestendig mogn gesein vnnd vnns aller der die wider vnns welten sein vnd In vntrew mainen, dester stattlicher mugn vffenthalten vnnd vnpillichs erwern vnd das wir auch manicherlay vnratz der wol Zu Ziten In etlichen Stetten geschechen ist, vertragen vnd absein vnd den als wir hoffen hierInn nutzlich Zufürkomen, So wöllend ditz nachfolgend schrift aigentlich vermerckn.' *Nördlingen Stadtarchiv Ordnungen*, Tumultordnungen 1481. The author's transcription differs somewhat in spelling from that of K. O. Müller, *Nördlinger Stadtrechte des Mittelalters*, Bayerische Rechtsquellen, Vol. ii (Munich, 1933), pp. 552–3.

22 In the sense of being related through legal bonds.

23 W. Ullmann, *Principles of Government and Politics in the Middle Ages* (London, 1961).

24 W. Stürner, 'Die Gesellschaftsstruktur und ihre Begründung bei Johannes von Salisbury, Thomas von Aquin and Marsilius von Padua', in A. Zimmerman (ed.), *Soziale Ordnungen im Selbstverständnis des Mittelalters*, Miscellanea Medievalia, Vol. xii/1 (Berlin and New York, 1979), pp. 162–78.

25 ibid, pp. 168 ff.

26 W. Mager (as in n. 14), p. 412.

27 W. Ullmann (as in n. 23), p. 133.

28 ibid., p. 134. W. Conze, 'Vom "Pöpel" zum "Proletariat": Sozialgeschichtliche Voraussetzungen für Sozialismus in Deutschland', *Vierteljahrsschrift für Sozial- und Wirtschaftsgeschichte*, xli (1954), 333–64, repr. in H. -U. Wehler (ed.), *Moderne deutsche Sozialgeschichte*, Neue Wissenschaftliche Bibliothek, Vol. x, 2nd edn (Cologne and Berlin, 1968), pp. 111–36.

29 W. Ullmann (as in n. 23), p. 217.

30 F. Keutgen (as in n. 15), p. 245: 'getruwe ind holt'.

31 J. Gény (ed.), *Schlettstadter Stadtrechte*, 2nd pt, Oberrheinische Stadtrechte, Vol. iii, Elsässische Stadtrechte, Vol. i (Heidelberg, 1902), p. 494: 'gehorsam'.

32 J. J. Moser, *Von der Reichs-Stättischen Regiments-Verfassung*, Neues teutsches Staatsrecht, Vol. xviii (Frankfurt and Leipzig, 1772; repr. Osnabrück, 1967), p. 73: 'Die Burgerschafft und übrige Eingesessene einer Reichstatt haben in Corpore und einzeln gegen die Obrigkeit eben diejenige Pflichten, wie anderer Reichsstände Unterthanen gegen ihre Landesherrschaft; nemlich 1. Ehrerbietigkeit und 2. Gehorsam.' For the following quotation see ibid., p. 96.

33 W. Ebel, *Der Bürgereid als Geltungsgrund und Gestaltungsprinzip des deutschen mittelalterlichen Stadtrechts* (Weimar, 1958).

34 J. J. Moser (as in n. 32), p. 76.

35 W. Ebel (as in n. 33), p. 24.

36 H. Fehr, 'Das Stadtvolk im Spiegel des Augsburger Eidbuches', in W. Fraenger (ed.), *Die Volkskunde und ihre Grenzgebiete*, Jahrbuch für historische Volkskunde, Vol. i (Berlin, 1925), pp. 39 and 47.

37 G. Oexle, 'Die mittelalterlichen Gilden: ihre Selbstdeutung und ihr Beitrag zur Formung sozialer Strukturen', in A. Zimmermann (ed.), *Soziale Ordnungen* (as in n. 24), pp. 203–26.

38 J. F. Boehmer (ed.), *Urkundenbuch der Reichsstadt Frankfurt* (Frankfurt/ Main, 1836), p. 101.

39 C. P. Clasen, *Anabaptism: a Social History, 1525–1618: Switzerland, Austria, Moravia, South and Central Germany* (Ithaca, NY and London, 1972), pp. 174–5, 181–2.

40 G. Müller (ed.), *Andreas Osiander d.Ä. Gesamtausgabe*, Vol. ii: Schriften und Briefe April 1525 bis Ende 1527 (Gütersloh 1977), no. 72, pp. 307 ff. Müller, *Reformation und Stadt: Zur Rezeption evangelischer Verkündigung*, Abhandlungen der geistes- und sozialwissenschaftlichen Klasse der Akademie Mainz 1981, Heft 11 (Wiesbaden, 1981), p. 25.

41 G. Oexle (as in n. 37), p. 213.

42 Aristotle, *Politics*, V.8. Here translated from the German version, ed. O. Gigon, dtv no. 6022 (Munich, 1973), p. 181.

43 E. Deuerlein, 'Ulrich Schwarz', in *Lebensbilder aus dem Bayerischen Schwaben*, Vol. ii (Munich, 1953), pp. 94–121. G. Panzer, *Ulrich Schwarz, der Zunftbürgermeister von Augsburg, 1442–1478*, phil. diss. (Munich, 1912; Bamberg, 1914).

44 'Chronik des Hector Mülich', in F. Roth (ed.), *Die Chroniken der schwäbischen Städte: Augsburg*, vol. iii, (as in n. 16), p. 260.

45 ibid., p. 261.

46 ibid., pp. 415 ff. (dated 1555). See G. Panzer (as in n. 43), pp. 5–6.

47 ibid.

48 E. Deuerlein (as in n. 43).

49 P. Dollinger, 'Die deutschen Städte im Mittelalter: die sozialen Gruppierungen', in H. Stoob (ed.), *Altständisches Bürgertum*, Wege der Forschung, no. 417 (Darmstadt, 1978), Vol. ii, pp. 288–9.

50 München, ASTA, Reichsstadt Nördlingen, Akten 992. For more detailed comments on these speeches, see H.-C. Rublack, *Eine bürgerliche Reformation: Nördlingen*, Quellen und Forschungen zur Reformationsgeschichte, Vol. 51 (Gütersloh, 1982).

51 For further information, see L. Müller, 'Beiträge zur Geschichte des Bauernkriegs im Ries und seinen Umlanden', *Zeitschrift des Historischen Vereins für Schwaben und Neuburg*, xv (1888), 23–160; xvii (1890), 1–152, 253–75. G. Franz, *Der Deutsche Bauernkrieg*, 10th edn (Darmstadt, 1976), pp. 212–16.

52 München, ASTA (as in n. 50).

53 L. Spengler, Ermanung und Undterweysung zu einem tugendhaften Wandel (Nuremberg, *c.* 1509/10; repr. Nuremberg, 1830), p. 28. I owe this reference to Dr Berndt Hamm (Tübingen).

54 ibid.: 'Dann was ist tewflischers beschwerlijchers oder schedlijchers, dann

widerwijllen gramschafft unnd uneinikeit. Dagegen auch was lieblichers holtzseligers unnd nutzlichers, dann fride und einikeit. Dhweil doch, wie wir durch tägliche erfarnheit sehen, durch friden und eintrechtikeit kleine ding hoch erhebt werden und wachsen. Aber grosse ding, gantze commun und oberkeiten durch zwitracht und unfriden, zu nichten werden und gantz vergeen.'

55 E. Schubert, *König und Reich: Studien zur spätmittelalterlichen deutschen Verfassungsgeschichte*, Veröffentlichungen des Max-Planck-Instituts für Geschichte, Vol. lxiii (Göttingen, 1979), p. 17.

56 München, ASTA, Reichsstadt Nördlingen, Akten 42, ad. 42. Luther's version: 'Ein jglich Reich so es mit jm selbs vneins wird/das wird wüste. Vnd ein jgliche Stad oder Haus/so es mit jm selbs vneins wird/mags nicht bestehen.' cf. H. Volz (ed.), *D. Martin Luther Biblia. Das ist die gantze Heilige Schrifft Deudsch auffs new zugericht*, 3 vols, dtv no. 6033, (Munich, 1974), Vol. iii, p. 1898.

57 Sallust, *Jugurtha*, 10. 6.

58 H. -C. Rublack, 'Nördlingen zwischen Kaiser und Reformation', *Archiv für Reformationsgeschichte*, lxxi (1980), 124–6.

59 München, ASTA, Reichsstadt Nördlingen, Akten 42, ad, 42.

60 ibid., ad 14b. As G. Oexle (cited in n. 37, p. 215) points out, fraternal love had been a norm of the guilds, deduced directly from the Christian 'caritas'. The appeal to this norm stressed the equality of the citizens, not obedience to authority.

61 'Vor allen dingen anrufen brüderliche lieb.'

62 'Brüderlich lieb nicht vergessen.'

63 For example, the 'Twelve Articles of the Peasants'. See G. Franz, *Quellen zur Geschichte des Bauernkriegs*, (Darmstadt, 1963), p. 177; Gaismair's 'Landesordnung', in J. Bücking, *Michael Gaismair: Reformer – Sozialrebell – Revolutionär*, Spätmittelalter und Frühe Neuzeit, Vol. iv (Stuttgart, 1978), p. 150.

64 W. Vogt, *Die bayerische Politik im Bauernkrieg und der Kanzler Dr. Leonhard Eck, das Haupt des schwäbischen Bundes*, (Nördlingen, 1883), p. 393.

65 H. Lutz (as in n. 5), 170.

66 C. Hegel (ed.), *Die Chroniken der fränkischen Städte: Nürnberg*, Vol. v, *Die Chroniken der deutschen Städte*, Vol. xi, 2nd edn (Göttingen, 1961), pp. 779–804.

67 R. Wetzel and L. Graf zu Dohna (eds), *Libellus de exsecutione aeternae praedestinationis*, Spätmittelalter und Reformation: Texte und Untersuchungen, Vol. xiv (Berlin, 1979).

68 ibid., p. 281: 'nim auch war, nemlich das der unsteten natur keine stete würkung und der zergenklichen natur keine bleibhafte ubung geburt. Derhalben hüt dich, das du kein menschlich werk ewigest, und merk, das allein got eignet handeln durch ein einige, stete handlung.'

69 Luther's version: 'Des Menschen hertz schlehet seinen weg an/Aber der HERR allein gibt/das er fort gehe'. See H. Volz (as in n. 56), Vol. ii, p. 1115.

70 C. Hegel (as in n. 66), p. 786: 'Dabei das gemain volk zum gepett vermanet und gott einhelligklich angerueffen wirt, auf das sein göttliche gnade inen soliche leut zu regenten wolle fürsetzen, die neben der weishait und dem verstant auch mit forcht gottes begabet seien, also das darnach die gemainen empter unter dieselben dapfern gottsfürchtigen männer und nicht die mänder under die empter außgethailt mogen werden.'

71 O. Brunner, 'Souveränitätsproblem und Sozialstruktur in den deutschen Städten der frühen Neuzeit', repr. in H. Stoob (ed.), *Altständisches Bürgertum* (as in n. 49), Vol. ii, p. 390.

72 This contradicts the possible criticism that Scheurl did not argue theologically when he wrote to Staupitz. cf. Scheurl's text in C. Hegel (as in n. 66), p. 791.

73 R. Postel, '"Van gehorsame der overicheit": Obrigkeitsdenken in Hamburg zur Zeit der Reformation', in F. Kopitzsch *et al.*, *Studien zur Sozialgeschichte des Mittelalters und der Frühen Neuzeit* (Hamburg, 1977), pp. 161, 168; idem, 'Obrigkeitsdenken und Reformation in Hamburg', *Archiv für Reformationsgeschichte*, lxx (1979), 169–201, here 173–4.

74 L. B. Pascoe, 'Nobility and ecclesiastical office in fifteenth century Lyons', *Medieval Studies*, xxxviii (1976), 322.

75 E. von Borries, 'Wimpheling "Germania"', in von Borries (ed.), *Wimpheling und Murner im Kampf um die ältere Geschichte des Elsasses*, Schriften des wissenschaftlichen Instituts der Elsaß-Lothringer im Reich, Vol. xvi (Heidelberg, 1926).

76 O. Herding, 'Pädagogik, Politik, Geschichte bei Jakob Wimpheling', *L'Humanisme Allemand (1480–1540)*XVIIIe Colloque International de Tours, Humanistische Bibliothek, 1, vol. xxxviii (Munich and Paris, 1979), p. 120.

77 E. von Borries, 'Wimpheling' (as in n. 75), p. 117. T. A. Brady, 'Wimpheling' (as in n. 14).

78 E. von Borries, 'Wimpheling' (as in n. 75), p. 149.

79 ibid., pp. 116 ff.

80 J. M. Kittelson, as quoted by T. A. Brady, jun., *Ruling Class, Regime and Reformation at Strasbourg, 1520–1555*, Studies in Medieval and Reformation Thought, Vol. xxii (Leiden, 1978), p. 18, n. 57.

81 The German version: 'das nit die gwaltigen den myndern, daß nit die Richen den Armen, daß nit die Edelen den gemeynen Man in einichen weg nit allein nit vndertrucken sunder ouch nit zu versmohen oder verachten vndertandent und daß kein Stadt den andern zu vertrucken oder zu myndern such.'

82 W. Schulze, *Reich und Türkengefahr im späten 16. Jahrhundert. Studien zu den politischen und gesellschaftlichen Auswirkungen einer äußeren Bedrohung* (Munich, 1978), pp. 63 f.

83 B. Moeller, 'Diskussionsbericht', in Moeller (ed.), *Stadt und Kirche im 16. Jahrhundert*, Schriften des Vereins für Reformationsgeschichte, no. 190 (Gütersloh, 1978), p. 181; Moeller, 'Stadt und Buch: Bemerkungen zur Struktur des reformatorischen Bewegung in Deutschland', in W. J. Mommsen (ed.), *Stadtbürgertum und Adel in der Reformation – The Urban Classes, the Nobility and the Reformation*, Veröffentlichungen des Deutschen Historischen Instituts, London, Vol. v (Stuttgart, 1979), pp. 28 f.; W. Ehbrecht, 'Köln – Osnabrück -Stralsund: Rat und Bürgerschaft hansischer Städte zwischen religiöser Erneuerung und Bauernkrieg', in F. Petri (ed.), *Kirche und gesellschaftlicher Wandel* (as in n. 2), p. 29. For reference to norms in cities of the Hanseatic League, see ibid., pp. 26, 28.

84 T. A. Brady, *Strasbourg* (as in n. 80), p. 25.

85 O. Brunner, *Land und Herrschaft*, 6th edn (Darmstadt, 1970), p. 133.

86 O. Feger (ed.), *Das Rote Buch*, Konstanzer Geschichts- und Rechtsquellen, Vol. i (Sigmaringen, 1949), p. 140.

87 F. Keutgen (as in n. 15), p. 80.

88 E. von Borries, 'Wimpheling' (as in n. 75), p. 117.

89 'Dann ein yeglichs Gut, so vil es gemeiner ist, so vil ist es Heiliger, so vil ist es auch Göttlicher, dann an dem ist die lutere Lieb, an dem wurt die veste Truw zu dem gemeynen Nutz bewärt.' This recurs in the *Tetrapolitana*. See B. Moeller (ed.), *Martin Bucers Deutsche Schriften*, Vol. iii, (Gütersloh, 1969), p. 65: 'Ideo nihil posse inter Christiani hominis officia haberi, quod rationibus proximi non aliquid momentum adferat atque eo quoque plus ex officio Christiano esse, quo plus inde vtilitatis ad proximos perueniat.'

90 K. O. Müller (ed.), *Nördlinger Stadtrecht des Mittelalters*, Bayerische Rechtsquellen, Vol. ii (Munich, 1933), p. 154.

91 L. Lenk, *Augsburger Bürgertum im Späthumanismus und Frühbarock, 1580–1700*, Abhandlungen zur Geschichte der Stadt Augsburg, Schriftenreihe des Stadtarchivs Augsburg, Vol. xvii (Augsburg, 1968), p. 41.

92 G. Müller (as in n. 40), p. 88.

93 R. Stupperich (ed.), *Martin Bucers Deutsche Schriften*, Vol. i, Frühschriften 1520–34 (Gütersloh, 1960), pp. 29–67.

94 ibid., p. 55.

95 Erasmus, 'Institutio principis christiani' in O. Herding (ed.), *Opera Omnia Desiderii Erasmi Roterdami*, Vol. iv/l (Amsterdam 1974), pp. 96 ff.

96 R. Stupperich (as in n. 93), p. 55.

97 O. Herding (as in n. 95), p. 55.

98 *Deutsches Rechtswörterbuch*, Vol. ii (Weimar, 1932), cols 1274 f. R. Scheyhing, 'Ehre', in *Handwörterbuch zur deutschen Rechtsgeschichte*, Vol. i (Berlin, 1971), col. 847.

99 See n. 8.

100 The Nuremberg Council stated: 'daß allein nutz wer der stat und gemain, das mit ern beschehe; und kain sach solt beschehen, wie groß nutz sie brecht, die unerlich wer.' See C. Hegel (ed.), *Die Chroniken der fränkischen Städte: Nürnberg*, Vol. iii, *Die Chroniken der deutschen Städte*, Vol. iii (Leipzig, 1884), p. 85.

101 Quoted according to E. Wolf (ed.), *Quellenbuch zur Geschichte der deutschen Rechtswissenschaft* (Frankfurt/Main, 1949), p. 34.

102 A.-K. Brandt, *Die 'tugentreich fraw Armut': Besitz und Armut in der Tugendlehre des Hans Sachs*, Gratia: Schriften der Arbeitsstelle für Renaissanceforschung am Seminar für Deutsche Philologie der Universität Göttingen, Vol. iv (Göttingen, 1979), p. 40.

103 ibid., p. 18: 'Auß dem so merck ein yeder man, Will er gemach und friede han, So meyd er wiederpörstig art Und halte für nicht wiederpart.'

104 'So leid als, was ein man ie liedt! Such weg zu einigkeyt und friedt.'

105 K. O. Müller (as in n. 90), pp. 63, 78, 140 and 291.

106 W. Kunkel (as in n. 7), pp. 514 f.

107 G. Müller (as in n. 40), p. 122.

108 E. P. Thompson, 'The moral economy of the English crowd in the eighteenth century', *Past and Present*, l (1971), 76–136.

109 V. Drehsen and H. J. Helle, 'Religiosität und Bewußtsein: Ansätze zu einer wissenssoziologischen Typologie von Sinnsystemen', in W. Fischer and W. Marhold (eds), *Religionssoziologie als Wissenssoziologie*, Urban paperback edn, no. 636 (Stuttgart, 1978), pp. 38 ff, esp. nn. 11 and 12 (containing references to A. Schütz, P. L. Berger and T. Luckmann).

110 H.-C. Rublack, 'Sozialtopographie' (as in n. 2), pp. 186–8, with further bibliographical references.

111 R. W. Scribner, 'Sozialkontrolle und die Möglichkeit einer städtischen Reformation', in B. Moeller (ed.), *Stadt und Kirche* (as in n. 83), pp. 57–65.

112 On unity as a norm in marital life, cf. A. van der Lee (ed.), *Marcus von Weida, Spiegel des ehlichen Ordens*, Quellen und Forschungen zur Erbauungsliteratur des späten Mittelalters und der frühen Neuzeit, Vol. i (Assen, 1972), pp. 23 and 29.

113 'Sunderliken to bedenckende unde vorttosetten dat ghemeyne ghut: wan dat gemeyne guth so flitligen geachtet worde, unde de oversten der stede sick under malckandere leyff hedden, ik befrochte my, dat got meyne twydracht ane twyvele der lete manghet komen. Over de egene nuth unde affgunst de is sere in den steden mangk den slechten, dat se partigeschen syn.' See *Die Chroniken der deutschen Städte, Vol. xvi: Braunschweig*, Vol. ii (Leipzig, 1880), p. 299 ('Das Schichtbuch'/*c*.1514).

3

Peasant Resistance in Sixteenth- and Seventeenth-Century Germany in a European Context

WINFRIED SCHULZE

One of the first attempts to survey the European peasant revolts of the sixteenth and seventeenth centuries was a study by the British historian, Henry Kamen. Kamen's evidence shows that a wide range of peasant resistance movements was occurring roughly contemporaneously throughout Europe, and that these movements peaked around the turn of the seventeenth century.[1] The extent of the movements is indicated by a few examples. There were the French Croquants' revolts in Limousin and Périgord (1593–5), the English revolts in Oxfordshire in 1596, the peasants' wars in Lower and Upper Austria between 1594 and 1597,[2] a few smaller revolts in Upper Swabia, Allgäu and Bavaria, on the Upper Rhine and in the Swiss Confederation, and individual revolts in Lusatia and Bohemia.[3] Central European observers undoubtedly perceived the danger of a new, far-reaching peasants' war. But revolts were also simmering outside western and central Europe, an area which had long been disturbed. In 1596 and 1597 there were uprisings in Finland, Poland, Russia and Lithuania. There is also evidence of revolts in Hungary in 1597, and in 1573 there were distinct signs of strong resistance to the feudal lords in southern Styria and in Croatia-Slavonia.[4]

The causes and aims of these movements varied, as did their scale, but taken together they point to the existence of peasant resistance as a regularly occurring phenomenon and one which at intervals culminated in revolts and wars. This must be seen as part of everyday life in the European states in the early modern period, although historical research to date has not dealt with it adequately, and only vague attempts have been made to see it as a phenomenon affecting the whole of Europe.[5] The French medievalist, Marc Bloch, observed that the peasant revolt was as integral to feudal society as the strike is to capitalist enterprise.[6]

Such a comparison involves obvious problems. Bloch left for future historians the task of investigating the conditions, forms and effects of peasant resistance and of fitting them into an overall historical context. How has historical research coped with this task? Has Bloch's assertion that resistance was normal been taken at all seriously?

A brief glance at the state of research on this topic shows that historians have only very recently begun to tackle the subject. Nineteenth-century historians naturally considered the peasant resistance movements from a monarchical point of view. They were interpreted as factors which hindered the development of the modern state, used as arguments in confessional or dynastic polemics and finally described as inexplicable modes of behaviour, as, for example, when Leopold von Ranke spoke of the German Peasants' War as the 'greatest natural event in the history of the German state'.[7] Historians whose outlook was coloured by governments' views settled for a few spectacular examples of peasant wars or revolts and adopted unquestioningly the official assessment of documents and the evidence of contemporary reports which referred to the rebellious people as a 'many-headed monster' or a '*beste farouche*'.[8] In any case such historians usually rejected in principle any research into movements which were likely to discredit the national dynasties.

Few nineteenth-century historians paid any attention to peasant resistance as a phenomenon *sui generis*. On the other hand, contemporaries of the seventeenth and eighteenth centuries regarded the revolts of the 'common man' as having a logic of their own. In his study on revolution and continuity in early modern Europe, John H. Elliott has pointed to the abundance of evidence which explains ideas on 'sedition' and 'rebellion'[9] and a later witness can also be cited, an anonymous author writing in 1785, who made a comparative study of the incidence of revolt in individual European countries (Hungary, Prussia, England, France) in the context of the relationship existing between ruler and subjects in each.[10] In view of this approach it is all the more surprising that no comparative research on revolts in Europe has been undertaken in the nineteenth and twentieth centuries.

It is beyond the scope of this article to discuss the various studies which do not conform to this pattern. In general terms it can be established that the social revolutions of the nineteenth century and the simultaneous emergence of Marxist-oriented movements provided the impetus for the long-neglected history of the peasant revolts to be researched more thoroughly and – above all – to be placed in a political context. Much the same applies to those revolts which were part of the formation of the European nation-states, and which can be politically assessed from this point of view. Attention should also be drawn to some of the research into rural history which was undertaken in the nineteenth century, and which has made the history of local and regional peasant revolts accessible to later generations of historians.[11]

Before surveying recent research, I want to discuss a terminological problem. Normally historians use the term 'peasant revolts' because it has proved to be a common denominator for the multifarious social movements amongst rural populations. But this does not take account of the fact that conceptually not all of these movements can be characterised as revolts in the narrower sense. A graded spectrum of peasant reaction to feudal or state demands has been developed for certain regions. Reactions range from the careless performance of statute labour, via litigation, organised withholding of dues and services and the use of violence in self-defence against state reprisals, to open revolt as the top rung on the scale of peasant resistance. This involved organised armed uprisings against towns, feudal manors, tax collectors or military detachments. Since this stage was exceptional rather than the rule in the peasants' struggle, 'revolt' can be defined as a peasant resistance movement on a local or regional level, making more or less concrete demands on the relationship between lords and peasants. Organisationally it was largely a defensive movement, that is organised violence was used only when the peasants' rights seemed to be threatened.[12]

Naturally enough, historical research initially concentrated on the most conspicuous forms of peasant wars and revolts. However, the varying degrees of peasant resistance in the examples I have detailed above seemed to call for intensive investigation of the whole gamut of conflicts between the state or landlords and peasants. It seems appropriate, therefore, to regard the revolts I shall be looking at here as one type within the broad spectrum of peasant resistance. Given the present state of research,[13] it is rather difficult to draw conclusions about the frequency of conflicts and internal social stability simply on the basis of the *number* of revolts and peasants' wars. Geoffrey Elton pointed out that the hundreds of minor uprisings and disturbances which occurred year after year were much more of a problem for the government of Tudor England than the major uprisings which happened only occasionally.[14] This observation on the internal structures of the early modern state also modifies the definition of revolt which can be discussed only briefly in this context. We still need comparative studies of the conflicting interests of landlords and peasants, of litigation, of interference by the central state authorities – in general, studies of the various forms in which conflict appeared and was resolved within the different socio-political systems.[15]

II

There is no doubt that present interpretations are decisively determined by the opposition between Marxist and non-Marxist approaches to history. The different internal situations in the eastern and south-eastern European countries and the unorthodox questions posed by western European Marxists have produced a relatively broad spectrum of partially overlapping approaches. Nevertheless, the basic Marxist – non-Marxist distinction remains a useful starting-point.

On the Marxist side every analysis of social conflicts in the era of feudalism must begin with the concept of class struggle introduced into recent research as a working concept by the Soviet historian B. F. Poršnev (although, of course, such terminology has a long tradition). Poršnev's most important methodological contribution was his adaptation of the concept of class struggle to fit the historical reality of the early modern period by introducing the term 'lower forms of class struggle'. At the same time Poršnev linked the peasants' 'class struggle' to the emergence of the state during this era. In short, according to his thesis peasant uprisings made the development of centralised national monarchies necessary; absolutism, as the most highly developed form of monarchical rule, was the obvious consequence of the peasants' struggle.[16]

As soon as Poršnev's thesis was published it provoked a heated debate which had far-reaching influence in eastern Europe and made a powerful impact on western research. The main accusation of his critics, made in discussion reports and counter publications, was that he hypostasised class struggle, elevating it to a 'law of development in feudal society'. J. A. Kosminski, Poršnev's strongest critic, argued that 'when Poršnev introduces the term class struggle to describe this development instead of referring to the increase in productive resources and the change in the modes of production, he robs the concept of class struggle of its historical basis, makes it into a supra-historical category and distorts the natural character of humanity's historical development'.[17] But despite these methodological criticisms, there is no doubt that Poršnev's differentiation of the concept of class struggle, and the connection he established between peasant resistance and absolutism, were widely accepted. They unquestionably influenced further research in this field. The distinction between the 'objective driving force' of productive resources and the 'subjective momentum' of class struggle made by the East German historian, Bernhard Töpfer, renders this thesis more acceptable.[18]

While the general meaning of the term class struggle was preserved, a methodological differentiation was attempted whereby additional features were specified in the hope of compensating for some of the shortcomings of this term. Nevertheless, it does not avoid one fundamental disadvantage of consistently using the term 'class struggle', namely that its universal application to the early modern period implies far too sharp a polarisation of the social interest groups involved. In fact, this polarisation is not evident in the revolts. The medievalist, Rodney Hilton, points out that the peasants had relationships with other social groups 'which inevitably generate antagonisms'.[19] This formulation suggests the possibility of differentiating not only between conflicting social interests, but also to discern the tensions, conflicts and solutions arising from them. This differentiation is necessary to explain social movements, but it is obscured by the concept of class struggle. Furthermore, the undifferentiated application of this concept involves underrating the role of the early modern state in developing new ways of resolving social conflict, ways which differed from those preferred by noble landowners.

Finally, French research has drawn attention to the difficulties caused by trying to apply the term 'class struggle' to a society whose system of values and scale of interests were essentially of a corporate nature.[20] Historians need to take account of these reservations, because the social conflicts of that era also produced vertical solidarities which do not adequately fit into the concept of class struggle. However, these critical reservations do not detract from the fact that the intensive research undertaken on peasant revolts in east-central and eastern Europe has resulted in many worthwhile collections of documents and individual analyses.

III

Non-Marxist research on the history of European peasant revolts is not dominated by any single overriding feature such as the concept of class struggle in the Marxist sphere. None the less, this concept provided an impetus which also affected research in the West, directly and indirectly.

This applies most clearly to historians working in French history. They had to come to terms not only with trends of Poršnev's research, but also with his survey of peasant resistance preceding the Fronde.[21] Poršnev cast doubt upon a model of the *ancien régime* that had previously been widely accepted by French historians – a model according to which the famous peasant revolts of the sixteenth and seventeenth centuries were seen primarily as uprisings by regional units against a centralised fiscal policy. As this controversy has received a great deal of attention, there is no need to discuss it any further here. Robert Mandrou suggests, however, that its impact should not be underestimated.[22] The long-term repercussions of the controversy between Poršnev and Roland Mousnier are of importance here. Despite the differences in their interpretations, both authors considered the peasant revolts as movements of great significance, without which the development of French absolutism could not be understood. The controversy led to intensive research into this aspect of the peasant revolts. It involved both those historians who, following Mousnier, stressed the anti-fiscal nature of the revolts,[23] and those who based their study of the revolts on intensive research into rural social structures, emphasised the changing modes of conflict, or were concerned with problems of organisation and the motives of the rebellious peasants.[24] All this raised further questions which still attract the interest of scholars in this field. They have also become important for research into the English peasant revolts. Clifford Davies has tested the results of this research using Mousnier's approach.[25] I shall leave aside for the moment Mousnier's question concerning the objectives of the peasants in revolt.

Non-Marxist research in the West has tended to concentrate on the following issues: first, how the movements were organised – a question of particular interest for comparative studies in social protest. It is, therefore, not surprising that certain attempts at a classification (for example, those by Berć, C. Tilly and Sabean) have used this criterion and have stressed the revolts' orientation towards communal concerns.[26]

The second issue – which is also relevant for comparative studies – concerns the motives behind the peasant resistance movements. In other words, what were their objectives? This touches on Mousnier's distinction between anti-fiscal and anti-feudal and also on the distinction drawn by C. Tilly between reactive and proactive versions of social protest. Using this distinction Tilly attempted to reassess the different objectives of the rebellious peasants of the seventeenth and the striking workers of the nineteenth centuries.[27]

The third issue concerns the legitimacy of the peasant movements. This is particularly important, because it locates the origins of peasant resistance in peasant attitudes and patterns of behaviour. It is no longer necessary to regard peasant revolts as an outbreak of elemental forces, or as an irrational form of behaviour – as is suggested by the use of such terms as *fureur paysanne* (Mousnier) or *force aveugle* (Pétran, Mandrou).[28] Various historians have examined and attempted to explain the behaviour of the lower classes, for example E. P. Thompson for the English lower classes in the eighteenth century, George Rudé for the *Sansculottes*, Natalie Zemon Davis for the religious unrest in sixteenth-century France,

Emmanuel Le Roy Ladurie for the peasants of Languedoc, to name but a few.[29] Even though their subjects vary widely, all these historians are attempting to trace the apparent irrationality of these resistance movements back to hitherto unrecognised patterns of social behaviour. A few years ago Natalie Zemon Davis emphasised the achievements of these historians when she pointed out that 'nowadays this hydra-headed monster has taken on a more orderly shape. ... We may see these crowds as prompted by political and moral traditions that legitimise and even prescribe their violence'[30]

IV

Comparative historical research must be aware of its limitations and the inherent dangers of getting bogged down in posing meaningless questions or of formulating trivialities. In our case, this means avoiding an approach which seeks to find a single explanation for peasant resistance valid for all European countries. There is no lack of historians who consider a comparative European approach problematic and who stress the uniqueness of the various movements.[31] The only way to make a comparative approach possible and meaningful is to examine the structural conditions of the revolts.

The following structural conditions can be established:

(1) In all European states the peasants comprised an overwhelming proportion of the population and their production formed the backbone of the national economies.
(2) In all European states the peasants thus formed the basis of the whole social system. Their taxes and dues financed a large proportion of the noble estates and the national budget.
(3) From the beginning of the sixteenth century to the end of the eighteenth century all European states were, to varying degrees, in a transitional phase between a subsistence

and a market economy. This accounts for the fact that in some countries 'islands of industrial activity' developed which, during commercial crises, were heavily dependent on the supply and price of grain.

(4) During this era all European states experienced rivalry between autonomous feudal lords and centralised or centralising monarchies. Both competed for control of the peasants.

These four conditions are likely to arouse particular interest in the reactions of the peasants to the process of change outlined above. They also provide us with the premises from which a general description of the system of interests that determined the relationship between peasants, landlords and early modern state can proceed. In the countries of early modern Europe state formation advanced very unevenly and in none of them was the peasant–landlord relationship as such a decisive factor. In all cases the national monarchies emerged – with greater or lesser intensity – as further power factors, even if only through their levying of taxes. Thus, a triangular relationship developed between peasants, feudal lords and the state authorities. It was determined by three groups of interests:

(1) In view of the growth of monetary exchange and generally favourable agrarian market conditions caused by upward demographic trends, the feudal lords were eager to make the best possible use of obligatory dues and services.

(2) The peasants were interested in securing as far as possible their individual and collective claims to land, their rights of inheritance and their rights to use or sell their products under favourable conditions. Only in this way could they make their individualised use of the land profitable and have a share in the market.

(3) The central monarchies (in Germany the territorial

states) had a major interest in an economically healthy population which was able to pay taxes. This enabled the rulers to assert themselves abroad and to stabilise their regimes at home.

If these general economic trends are accepted as valid, then the most important consequence resulting from the divergent interests of peasants, landlords and central authorities appears to be that certain fundamental conflicts were unavoidable. With increased production for the market, conflict between peasants and landlords over the optimal use of market opportunities was inevitable. This accounts for the landlords' imposition of the *Anfallzwang* (compulsory sale of the peasants' products), the increase in compulsory services, the enclosure movement and expropriation of the peasants, as well as the peasants' refusal to perform services and their struggle against the landlords' privileges. At the same time it became obvious that in a society structured along these lines the traditional functional system of balanced duties and rights was bound to collapse. The basis of what George Duby called a static *société tripartite* or *trifonctionelle* was called into question – a process which had significant consequences.[32]

The divergence of the interests of peasants, landlords and princes was obviously one of the most prominent features of the European states in the early modern period. This period of European history is characterised by two levels of internal conflict: *Ständekämpfe*, *frondes*, conflicts between princes and parliaments on the one hand, and peasant revolts on the other. Sometimes these two types of conflict coincided chronologically, for example in the Habsburg territories at the end of the sixteenth century when disputes between princes and estates over confessional matters overlapped with peasant wars. The same applies to the French peasant revolts of the sixteenth and seventeenth centuries when the throne had to assert its authority against both aristocratic regionalism and peasant resistance.[33] Both levels of conflict can be traced back to the constellation of interests outlined above. The main bone of contention during the *Ständekämpfe* was the right to levy taxes, and early parliamentary assemblies' support for this right. In the peasant revolts, on the other hand, the main issue was the degree of taxation and the various forms of exacting rent. To be more precise: in the *Ständekämpfe* the fundamental right to seize the peasants' produce was disputed; in the peasant revolts it was the *extent* to which the peasants' produce could be channelled away which was at issue. It seems to me that it is necessary to see the connection between these two levels of conflict more clearly than has been done to date. Research into parliamentary assemblies, which hitherto has been pursued mainly on an institutional level, ought, therefore, to be combined with research into the history of the peasant resistance movements.[34]

Comparative European research into 'Parliaments, Estates and Representation' has achieved much.[35] Similar research into peasant revolts of the early modern period should be regarded as equally appropriate and useful. The various types of peasant resistance in the European states indicate the degree of internal social stability. Let us assume that the development of the modern states of Europe and their specific attempts to establish internal stability were a reaction to a multitude of organisational problems of an economic, social and religious nature. It should be obvious that resistance by the peasants, precisely that section of the population which formed the backbone of the state in this period, is an excellent starting-point for assessing the success or failure of early state-building and the process by which it was implemented.

Peasant resistance should also be seen in the context of the general process of transition from a feudal to a bourgeois capitalist system. This transition may be seen as the result of the agrarian sector being taken over by commercial or industrial modes of production, by a victorious market-oriented, commercialised agriculture, or by a regionally differentiated 'agrarian capitalism'.[36] In any case, peasant reaction to this fundamental transition counteracted this process. According to E. J. Hobsbawm, it can be established 'with some probability' that 'from the sixteenth to the eighteenth century the successful resistance of the peasants did indeed slow down the development towards capitalism'.[37] The general validity of such a statement might still be disputed, but the suggestion that peasant resistance should be included as a factor in this process of transformation is useful. This process is all too often dealt with only in terms of objective economic factors. The starting-point for the discussion about the transition from feudalism to capitalism is the Dobb–Sweezy debate on the 'endogenous' or 'exogenous' nature of this process. In 1977 the American historian, Robert Brenner, re-emphasised the role of social conflict in this debate by discussing demographic theories of development (M. M. Postan, E. Le Roy Ladurie).[38] Relating peasant resistance to the process of transition does not merely link economic and structural changes with social conflicts, it also takes account of the role of the early modern state as a levier of taxes and regulator of conflicts, a role which Brenner underestimates.

Acknowledging a relationship between peasant resistance movements and economic and political stability means that the rebellious behaviour of peasants can no longer be regarded as an isolated phenomenon. Nor should we be excessively concerned with hair-splitting distinctions between different forms of peasant resistance. Rather, we should focus on the reactions of the peasant classes to the processes of modernisation in agrarian production, to the increasing demands of the landlords, to the modern state's tax demands and to its intensified exercise of power. Analysis of the peasant resistance movements can thus contribute to an in-depth examination of the emergence of the early modern political and social system. This might also meet the criticism made as early as 1958 by the British historian, David Pennington, who expressed his astonishment at the fact that historians researching early modern Europe,[39] which was characterised by general unrest, have always looked for the causes of revolts and not for the reasons why they failed or why the traditional order survived.

V

Pennington's criticism also suggests that the different frequency and the chronology of the revolts in the various European countries deserve further investigation. It might be possible to establish a connection between the frequency of peasant revolts and the level of social and political development of the territories in which they occurred.

A brief look at the chronological sequence of peasant revolts in western Europe makes it clear that in France and England the revolts came in relatively clearly defined cycles. In the case of France E. Le Roy Ladurie, in agreement with other historians, considers the period from 1548 (Pitauds' Uprising against the Gabelle in Guyenne) to 1675 (*papier timbré* uprising in Brittany)[40] to be a cycle of classical peasant revolts. Within this cycle, 1548 can be seen as the 'mother revolt'. It has been described as an anti-fiscal uprising and is summed up in the rebels' slogan 'Long live the King, but without the Gabelle'.[41] The year 1675 may well not have been the definitive end of this type of revolt. However, Le Roy Ladurie has sufficient evidence to support his thesis that between 1675 and 1685 the absolutist system was consolidated, namely that taxation, in real terms, decreased, that the confessional conflict was forcibly resolved (revocation of the Edict of Nantes) and that the intendants were more effectively able to stand up for the peasants.[42]

In England a comparable cycle can be observed extending from the revolts in Cornwall of 1497 to the agrarian revolts between 1628 and 1632.[43] Three distinct types of revolt occurred here: anti-fiscal revolts (characteristic of the early sixteenth century), revolts against the Reformation (parallel to the breakthrough of the Reformation and the dissolution of the monasteries around the middle of the century) and anti-seigneurial revolts, such as occurred in 1549, 1607 and 1628–32. These revolts were obviously reactions to the three fundamental processes of modernisation – the extension of fiscal policy, the Reformation and the 'agrarian revolution', that is the commercialisation of agrarian modes of production by, for example, the establishment of enclosures and moorland drainage[44].

These cycles of revolts in England and France were both followed by 'food riots' or *révoltes frumentaires*, that is, unrest arising from the discrepancy between wages and the cost of foodstuffs.[45] No comparable phenomenon can be found in central and eastern Europe. The great wave of peasant wars in this area in the late fifteenth and early sixteenth centuries can by no means be considered the end of a cycle. At the end of the sixteenth and beginning of the seventeenth century a new wave of revolts occurred in the Upper German and Habsburg regions. And even this was not the end of it. Throughout the whole of this period we find a continuous series of resistance movements, which do not form clearly defined cycles. The forms they took varied considerably: they can be classified only in terms of the different territories in which they occurred. The same is true of east-central and south-eastern Europe, where, as in central Europe, revolts against the feudal system predominated, although there were some fiscal revolts as well. Viktor Buganov speaks of a 'relative delay' in Russia, where peasant uprisings did not reach their peak until the seventeenth and eighteenth centuries. This can be explained by the 'delayed' capitalist development in Russia, and by the fact that absolutism only then began to develop.[46] Josef Petran has shown that the same argument applies to Poland and Bohemia, where peasant movements did not reach their climax until the second half of the eighteenth century.[47]

If these findings are accepted, at least in broad outline, then relatively clearly defined cycles of revolts can be observed in

England and France, running parallel to the great processes of state and economic modernisation in these countries (the Reformation, the commercialisation of agriculture, increased taxation, the emergence of absolutism). On the other hand, no clearly defined cycle is discernible for central, east-central and south-eastern Europe. Here it was much more a question of change in the forms of protest, or of a series of resistance movements without any clearly recognisable periodisation. The particular features of these movements can be related only to the specific social and political conditions in the territorial states of the Holy Roman Empire and the Habsburg lands (Bohemia and Hungary with Slavonia and Croatia included).

The different time sequence of the revolts suggests that these movements should be seen in the context of the process of European state formation. This process involved the development of a centralised administration, a comprehensive taxation system, one national denomination, and clearly defined relations of power between parliaments and princes. This new stage in state organisation was associated with strong resistance from the estates and with peasant revolts. In this broader perspective, the revolts were an important indicator of the extent, duration and success of the process of modernisation,[48] and peasant resistance also helped to determine the direction of this development.

A second observation, regarding the scope of the resistance movements, follows from the above. Revolts against the process of state modernisation had far greater scope than anti-seigneurial revolts. Resistance to fiscal policy or to reform 'from above' naturally extended further than the specific problems of individual landlords. Feudal disputes clearly required a recognisable common anti-peasant policy – a condition which was on the whole difficult to fulfil, as the English enclosure movement and the Bohemian compulsory labour policy illustrate. Generally, however, anti-seigneurial movements were organised on a local or manorial, or at most regional level, while the scope of the anti-state or anti-fiscal revolts was much broader.

Finally, I would like to make a few remarks on the historiography of peasant resistance in Germany. Not much research has been done on this in Germany and even less is known about it elsewhere.[49] There is a historiographical gap in the literature available in English on the period between the end of the great Peasants' War in 1526 and the German Jacobins. This gap reflects the state of recent German research. The picture which emerges from this research is one of a politically apathetic peasantry, especially because emphasis is always laid on the section of Germany east of the Elbe which Western Europeans so often consider on its own.[50] Historical reality is considerably different. The Peasants' War was a trauma felt deeply by the aristocratic world,[51] but it was not the end of peasant resistance. As early as 1532 the peasants of Hüttenstein near Salzburg were planning to 'do it better' than they had done in 1525–6.[52] There were revolts in Lower Lusatia and a series of mostly regional or local revolts occurred,[53] culminating in a great wave of peasant wars in the Habsburg lands at the end of the sixteenth and beginning of the seventeenth century. An Austrian historian has described this as the 'long-term social tremor' of this era.[54] A series of smaller revolts took place at the same time in the regions between the Upper Rhine and the Allgäu. These were directed primarily against high imperial taxation and a general intensification in the policy of territorial state-building of the lesser dukes and lords between 1580 and 1620.

The Thirty Years' War generated various forms of rural defensive action. It was significant for peasant resistance in that the increased taxes and dues enforced during the war gave rise to new protest movements at the end of the war. There is evidence of this in Kempten and other Swabian domains and in the western and central German territories. In the county of Schönburg the conflict intensified into a dispute that lasted for years.[55]

Several smaller revolts occurred during the eighteenth century, but the exact number is difficult to establish. There were certainly no less than fifty individual rebellions in about thirty territories of the empire.[56]. They broke out primarily in the smaller territories of the empire and generally resulted in year-long trials at the highest imperial courts. These rebellions were related to issues which had long assumed central importance: fiscal policy and demands for dues and compulsory services. The extent of the rebellions is illustrated by the virtually continuous struggle by the serfs of Hohenzollern-Hechingen against their princely lords. In 1798 this finally led to a *Landes-Vergleich*, a quasi-constitutional agreement which shows the political potential of this movement.[57] This result is not unique. Indeed, most of the revolts were brought to an end by a treaty concluded between the prince and his peasant subjects. Even dynastic histories written from the point of view of the authorities in this period, such as were compiled in Sayn-Wittgenstein, Nassau-Weilburg, Kriechingen, Isenburg-Büdingen and in many houses of the imperial knights, cannot avoid comprehensively reporting these revolts. In the territory of the lords of Riedesel – to take just one example – the second half of the eighteenth century was a period of 'increasing rebelliousness amongst the serfs'. This greatly restricted the activity of the governmental apparatus.[58]

A purely chronological survey of the numerous local and regional revolts and resistance movements risks leaving movements of this kind unexplained. This approach suggests that the interest of historians in these movements is restricted to their regional effects, overlooking their wider political and social implications. Indeed, at first sight, the economic, social and political conditions under which revolts occurred and the forms which they took seem too varied to produce a coherent pattern such as has been established for France in the model of the 'anti-fiscal' revolts.[59]

These well-founded reservations have influenced research in

this field. Nevertheless, certain underlying tendencies can be discerned in the history of the peasant revolts between the Peasants' War and the French Revolution. First there is an obvious cluster of revolts in the Upper German area. The Upper Rhine, the Black Forest, Upper Swabia and the Habsburg lands undoubtedly experienced the greatest frequency of resistance and these revolts were also the most extreme. On the other hand, the frequency of revolts in the western, northern and eastern territories was much lower. In the central German area most revolts occurred in the seventeenth and eighteenth centuries.

These regional divisions are significant, because they reflect the extent of the Peasants' War of 1524–6. Nevertheless, a more useful approach is to assess whether there is a correlation between the size of the territorial states involved and the frequency of the uprisings. Even at first sight it is striking that the smaller territories were more seriously affected by revolts than the medium-sized or larger ones. This is illustrated by the revolts which took place in the following areas: Upper Germany (1580–1620), Solms-Greifenstein and Solms-Braunfels (1650–1729), the county of Schönburg (1650–81), Greiz (1714–30), Anhalt-Bernburg (1752), Schwarzburg-Rudolstadt (1627, 1716–36), Schaumburg-Lippe (1784–93), the counties of Sayn-Wittgenstein (1697–1725), Nassau-Weilburg and Isenburg-Meerholz (1718–73), the Bishopric of Kempten (1666–7 and 1721–31), the knights' estates at Illereichen (1653–61), the estate at Triberg in the Black Forest (1642–54),[60] the county of Hauenstein ('Saltpeter' disturbances) and the Hohenzollern counties in the eighteenth century. Numerous other examples could be cited, particularly if we include the procedural disputes of the eighteenth century. Our analysis of the published sources leads to the conclusion that smaller territories were more susceptible to revolts than larger ones.[61] This conclusion is supported by evidence drawn from the judgements of the *Reichshofrat* and of the highest imperial courts (which have not yet been thoroughly investigated).

But the size of a territory does not seem to be the only significant variable. In the territories most affected the prince played the dual role of sovereign and largest landowner, and there were no landed estates which could mediate between the prince and his subjects. On the other hand, territories, such as Lusatia,[62] whose estates were so strong that they could hardly be controlled, were equally susceptible to revolts. Thus my original thesis must be modified: territories in which the 'modern military, economic administrative state'[63] had not yet emerged, or not emerged fully, were most likely to suffer revolts.

These territories did not possess a strong administrative apparatus and a legal system which might have mediated between the peasants and the princes. These territories were also under greater financial pressure than larger ones, because of the unfavourable balance between the size of the population and government expenditure. This in turn was caused by the considerable financial burden of boundary divisions, testamentary contracts and compensation agreements and by the fact that imperial and regional taxes levied in these small territories were higher than they could bear. This provided favourable conditions for interference by the imperial authorities – a sign of internal weakness which the subjects were quick to recognise and to exploit.[64]

Any explanation of the German revolts must emphasise this last factor. It is quite clear that the majority of the revolts in the sixteenth, seventeenth and eighteenth centuries would not have taken place had the structure of the system of domination in the Holy Roman Empire been different. Several factors operated against the efforts of individual princes to exploit their subjects beyond the levels set by tradition: competition between minor, middling and great princes, rivalry between the ecclesiastical and secular authorities, rivalry between the towns and the landed nobility, and the political watch-dog role of the important imperial estates, such as the House of Habsburg in Upper Germany or the leading princes of the different *Kreise*. Finally, the emperor, the court and the high imperial law courts in Speyer, Wetzlar, Prague and Vienna formed extremely attractive focal points for peasants' complaints.[65] The German revolts of this period to some extent transcended the particular territory involved and, in the process of their development, appealed to external powers. This structure of domination gave the subjects a certain amount of elbow-room which they exploited and manipulated in an amazingly knowledgeable way. The evidence available supports the view that peasants' organisations were well aware of the political opportunities provided by this system of overlapping forms of domination and that they made them the basis of their calculations.

How else can the routes taken by peasant delegations be explained? One delegation, for example, went to Innsbruck, the seat of the highest Austrian government of the *Vorlande*, and from there to Prague to the imperial court.[66] How else can the conduct of a peasant community be explained which considered it advantageous to blacken the name of its lord in front of the emperor and the imperial diet in Regensburg? This community carefully considered whether to take its case to the Imperial Supreme Court (*Kammergericht*) or whether to wait for the establishment of an imperial commission.[67] Peasant communities also appealed to university faculties of law and their widely differing *rationes decidendi*.[68] Thus there was a considerable degree of intervention in these conflicts by 'external powers'.[69]

Our provisional theory which postulates an affinity between underdeveloped territorial states and the frequency of revolts, does, however, have one shortcoming: it by no means encompasses *all* the revolts of which we know. Even if historical models of explanation are not expected to be perfect, it is obvious that the Bavarian uprisings of 1633–4 and 1705–6 and the Austrian uprisings of 1596–7 and 1626 do not fit into this model.

However, Lower and Upper Austria would appear to be

special cases. They had special confessional problems, to which the 'foreign rule' of the Bavarians was added in 1626.[70] The Thirty Years' War (1633–4) and the occupation of the territory by imperial troops (1705–6)[71] also imposed a heavy burden upon the peasants. For the time being, the theory that there was a correlation between the relative backwardness of the governmental system and the likelihood of revolts allows us to put the German peasant revolts of the period under consideration into a general perspective. Peasant resistance is not merely linked in an abstract way to modes of production on which the feudal system is based, that is, compulsory rent for the use of land. The thesis developed here is more concerned with relating the mode of production to the system of government, thereby encompassing the whole framework of changing conditions which played a part in peasants' resistance. This includes the momentum created by local traditions and the generally accepted conceptions of liberty and rule.

This initial explanation of the causes of the German revolts in terms of the imperial system and the specific conditions of rule in the small territories must be supplemented by the examination of a much more fundamental feature of peasant resistance. I should like to define this as a *Verrechtlichung* (juridification) of the relationship between subjects, landlords and rulers which was brought about by the increasing importance of conflict resolution by litigation.[72] Eighteenth-century imperial lawyers were aware of the significance of the outcome of the Peasants' War for the emergence of the judicial constitution of the Holy Roman Empire; a more detailed examination of its political repercussions is likely to support this conclusion.[73] A comparative study of European peasant resistance reveals that the Peasants' War resulted not only in the princes' taking greater precautions against new revolts and in more severe levels of punishment, but also in more opportunities for the peasants to lodge complaints within the framework of the emerging territorial legal system. Similar tendencies related to legal reform can be found neither in Hungary after the Dozsa Uprising of 1514 nor in France after the Gabelle Uprising. In Hungary the peasants' *glebae udscriptio* was introduced and their opportunities for making complaints generally curtailed.[74] In England, for example, there was no reaction, after Somerset's failure, to the crisis of 1548–9, even if we take into account the commission of inquiry established to look into the enclosure problem and the long-term improvement in the copy-holder's right to sue.[75]

This argument about the 'juridification' of social conflicts in the Holy Roman Empire can draw upon a wide range of empirical evidence. Only a few aspects can be discussed here. First, the subjects' right to sue their princes was definitively secured by the Supreme Court ruling of 1555.[76] Secondly, the establishment of imperial commissions indicates that there was a trend towards diverting impending conflicts into forms of political resolution.[77] Thirdly, the clearest evidence of the emergence of 'juridification' is provided by the numerous law suits lodged by the peasants in the territorial and imperial courts. There were cases which were pending for generations. During this period there was hardly a revolt which did not have a parallel court case – indeed, the opportunities for resolving conflicts by litigation largely determined the tactics of the peasants' resistance. Finally, a special kind of literature on feudal rights provides evidence for the process of 'juridification'. Apart from literature on sedition, which was clearly more practically oriented than its French and English counterparts,[78] there are numerous essays on peasant dues, legal positions and services. These essays highlight the issues on which communities and landlords came into conflict.[79] Reference is continually made to the numerous court cases dealing with disputed services and dues, but the concept of 'legitimate resistance' against overburdening by the landlords also emerges clearly. The *saevitia dominorum* becomes a collective term for abuses by the landlords or princes and establishes grounds for criticism. The subjects had a precisely defined range of means of legal recourse against this *saevitia*, known as the *remedia juris*.[80]

This provides a link with the objectives and legitimation of resistance by the peasants. E. P. Thompson has suggested a concept of legitimation that has become widely accepted in European research.[81] A distinction must be made, however, between the legitimation of resistance by the English lower classes in the eighteenth century and by the German peasants in the early modern period. The English lower classes were dependent on the market economy ('moral economy'), while the German peasants were at least partly producers. If Thompson's concept is applied to the German sources, it becomes clear that *der bauern aigen sach and nahrung* (the peasants' property and subsistence) was the most important issue as far as the peasants were concerned. If the landlords encroached upon the peasants' traditional means of subsistence, the *mutua obligatio* was destroyed and resistance became legitimate. Historians have tended to find within Germany's past an allegedly characteristic attitude of submissiveness. In view of this, it seems particularly important to demonstrate and emphasise the existence of a generally accepted concept of socially legitimised resistance in this period.[82]

In conclusion, I should like to draw attention to the historical consequences of peasant resistance. First, it is difficult to repudiate the judgement, often and competently made, that the peasants' struggle was in fact tragically pointless.[83] Jean Jacquart has pointed to the 'failure of the peasants' resistance' in sixteenth- and seventeenth-century France[84] and John H. Elliott has asked the 'apparently brutal question' whether the innumerable peasant revolts made 'any difference' or could have made any difference 'in a world in which technological backwardness had at least as much to do with the condition of the populace as exploitation by an oppressive ruling class?'[85] On the other hand, Poršnev's thesis about the intrinsic connection between the peasant movements and the development of European absolutism does not seem to me to do justice to the complicated network of causes and effects associated with this phenomenon. Elliott's suggestion that the precise areas in which these movements gave rise to eventual change should be determined thus seems to indicate an appropriate line of inquiry.[86]

In some respects peasant resistance was partially successful. It led to the withdrawal of new taxes and of certain forms of taxation. It produced tax rebates and brought about the establishment of commissions of inquiry and the dismissal of dishonest officials, and so on. All this supports the general conclusion that peasant resistance movements of the early modern period led to the formation of a basic social consensus. Because peasants had little or no opportunity to participate in political processes, their will was expressed through resistance movements, which also revealed the extent to which the feudal order was considered justified. Thus, in spite of a few factors which lay beyond their control and gave these movements a certain dynamic of their own, they cannot be considered irrational.[87] They were based on the clear and generally accepted idea that subjugation had to be kept within certain limits and they were seen as giving expression to an at least passive consensus among the subjects. The burden imposed by dues and taxes could not be allowed to go beyond limits determined by the peasants' physical means of existence and social organisation. Yves-Marie Bercé demonstrates that the Croquants' resistance was to a considerable extent successful.[88] This is confirmed by an observation from the 'other side of the fence': long-term resistance (that is refusal of taxes, rents or compulsory labour) was increasingly regarded as an acceptable argument in the higher echelons of the political system. When the Bishop of Basel apologised to the emperor in 1580 for having entered into an alliance with the Swiss Confederation, he referred to the growing disobedience of his subjects and gave his assurance that he stood to gain a better rapport with his subjects as an ally of the Confederation.[89]

In his recent book on the end of the *ancien régime* in Europe,

Jerome Blum describes the effect of the peasant disturbances of the eighteenth century as follows: they 'penetrated the consciousness of the ruling classes', who became aware of the danger to their life and property and were, therefore, willing to accept a curtailment of their privileges.[90] The economic consequences of resistance can also be demonstrated. Peasant resistance led to a decrease in agrarian productivity and was closely connected with the transition from feudal services to paid work.

Finally, I should like to emphasise that peasant revolts in the early modern period played an important part in the political and economic development of the European countries, in as much as they influenced the speed of modernisation in state and economy. Governments' new judicial institutions and legal procedures developed regulating mechanisms in response to peasant rebellions. Privileges were abolished and attempts made to discipline the aristocracy. Peasant rebellions also led to a reform of the legal status of peasants and of land ownership. Francis Bacon's tract 'On sedition and troubles' provides an excellent illustration of these results. Under the heading of '*remedia praeservativa*', he discusses substantial reform measures such as the encouragement of industry and commerce, taxes against luxury goods, moderate taxation, the establishment of a numerical balance between nobility and common people, a reduction in the number of clerics and the prevention of monoplies and huge estates, 'for the surest way to prevent sedition (i.e. the times to bear it) is to take away the matter of them'. Bacon's tract seems to be a fairly reliable account of the issues which concerned the European ruling élites.[91] They were under the impression that, as the cameralist Johann Jakob Becher put it,[92] one rebel was worse than ten external enemies.

A comment made by Emperor Leopold II gives a clear impression of the range of the peasant movements' potential effects. In 1778 as Grand Duke of Tuscany, he investigated new measures to protect the peasants in Bohemia and wrote to his mother:

> and so a mass uprising by the peasants will be of use to the state by humbling the rulers and making them treat their peasants justly and fairly. The peasant class is as much a part of the monarchy as that of the landlords and they must all be protected and supported by, the government.[93]

The validity of this observation could be questioned on the grounds that it is an expression of princely cynicism. It is important to show, therefore, that such thoughts on reforming peasant conditions through revolts were being discussed at the court of Vienna even earlier in the eighteenth century. In 1705 Christian Schierl von Schierendorf, a councillor of the *Hofkammer*, thought it useful to propose a 'general convocation' of all the estates of the monarchy including a delegation representing the 'common man'. In the context of this proposal, the councillor also reflected on peasant rebellions, especially in Hungary. He concluded that if the Hungarian nobility were to reverse a reduction in peasant duties,[94] it could be helpful for the central government to instigate peasant rebellions. If we compare such eighteenth-century proposals with the reactions of frightened nobles and governments of the sixteenth century, it is obvious that peasant rebellions had acquired a different meaning. In the sixteenth century peasant rebellions were seen as dangerous events and always regarded as starting-points for a 'general and universal uprising of the subjects'.[95] Eighteenth-century rulers and political thinkers – such as Johann Heinrich von Justi, writing in 1756 – were aware that standing armies and political and social reforms had reduced the frequency of rebellions.[96] We are confronted once again with the ambiguous effects produced by peasant rebellions. They provoked a tightening of repression and control and, at the same time, led to political, social and economic reforms.

Peasant resistance in early modern Europe, therefore had significant consequences, although these differed in nature and extent from country to country; it regulated the exercise of noble and state power, led to its rationalisation and eventually weakened it. Peasant resistance must be seen as contributing to the European tradition which established the necessity of legitimising governmental control.[97] Feudal order as understood today always provided a starting-point for resistance against tyranny and the unjust behaviour of rulers. But resistance was not confined to the nobility and early parliamentary assemblies, or more generally, to the sphere of *dominium politicum et regale.*[98] Resistance also served the 'common people', whose historical importance emerges more clearly in this wider context than in the isolated analysis of a few great peasant wars which were quickly suppressed.

Notes: Chapter 3

This is an extended version of a paper presented to the seminar of the German Historical Institute London in June 1980. I would like to thank Professor Wolfgang J. Mommsen and the British colleagues who were present for a long and very helpful discussion. The translation was prepared by Miss Jane Williams of the Institute. The paper is a first result of a research project supported by the Stiftung Volkswagenwerk which concentrates on certain aspects of European agrarian conflicts from the fourteenth to the eighteenth centuries. The project is being carried out by Professor Peter Blickle (University of Bern) and myself. For other publications which have grown out of this project see notes 3, 5 and 48.

1 H. Kamen, *The Iron Century: Social Change in Europe 1550–1660* (London, 1971), pp. 365 ff.

2 Y.-M. Bercé, *Croquants et Nu-Pieds: les soulèvements paysans en France du XVIe au XIXe siècle* (Paris, 1974); Public Record Office London, State Papers 12, vols cclxi and cclxii; H. Feigl, *Der niederösterreichische Bauernaufstand 1596/97* (Vienna, 1972), and K. Eichmeyer, H. Feigl, R. W. Litschel, *Weilß gilt die Seel und auch das Guet: Oberösterreichische Bauernaufstände im 16. und 17. Jahrhundert* (Linz, 1976).

3 For detailed references see W. Schulze, *Bäuerlicher Widerstand und feudale Herrschaft in der frühen Neuzeit*, Neuzeit im Aufbau, Vol. vi (Stuttgart, 1980), pp. 49 ff. and additionally, for the Swiss Confederation, F. Meyer (ed.), 'Andreas Ryff (1550–1603), Der Rappenkrieg', *Basler Zeitschrift für Geschichte und Altertumskunde*, lxvi (1966), 5–131.

4 References are to be found in the volumes cited in nn. 18 and 5 by G. Heitz *et al.*, and G. Heckenast, and in S. Fischer-Galati, 'The peasantry as a revolutionary force in the Balkans', *Journal of Central European Affairs*, xxiii (1963), 12–22, and in H. Ylikangas, 'Die langfristigen Entwicklungstrends der Verbrechen

wider das Leben in Finnland', in *Rapports du XVe Congrès International des Sciences Historiques*, Vol. ii (Bucharest, 1980), pp. 690–704, here p. 697. For 1573, see W. Schulze, 'Der Windische Bauernaufstand von 1573: Bauernaufstände und feudale Herrschaft im späten 16. Jahrhundert', *Südost-Forschungon*, xxxiii (1974), 15–61.

5 The following comparative works have been published to date: S. Pascu, V. V. Mavrodin, B. F. Poršnev, J. G. Antelava, 'Mouvements paysans dans le centre et dans le sud-est de l'Europe du XVe au XXe siècle', in *Comité des Sciences Historiques: Rapports IV* (Vienna, 1965), pp. 211–35; R. Mousnier, *Fureurs paysannes: les paysans dans les révoltes du XVIIe siècle* (Paris, 1967). For a critique of the English translation of this book (1971) see *Past and Present*, li (1971), 63–80; H. A. Landsberger, 'The role of peasant movement and revolts in development', in Landsberger, *Latin American Peasant Movements* (Ithaca, NY and London, 1969), pp. 1–61; B. Moore, *Soziale Ursprünge von Demokratie und Diktatur: Die Rolle der Grundbesitzer und Bauern bei der Entstehung der modernen Welt* (Frankfurt/Main, 1974), esp. pp. 520 ff. L. Makkai, 'Periodisation und Typologie der europäischen Bauernbewegungen', in *U povadu 400. godisnýce hrvatsko-slovenske seljacke bune*, Radoviv (Zagreb, 1973), pp. 41–8; M. E. François, 'Revolts in late medieval and early modern Europe: a spiral model', *Journal of Interdisciplinary History*, v (1974), 19–43; the articles by Cistozvonow and Petran in G. Heitz *et al.* (eds), *Der Bauer im Klassenkampf*, (Berlin-East, 1975), pp. 1–26 and 449–67; D. Sabean, 'Markets, uprisings and leadership in peasant societies (Western Europe 1381–1789)', *Peasant Studies Newsletter*, ii (1973), 17–19; Ch. Tilly, 'Hauptformen kollektiver Aktion in Westeuropa 1500–1975', *Geschichte und Gesellschaft*, iii (1977), 153–63; V. Buganov, 'Bauernaufstände und Bauernkriege in Ost-, Mittel- und Westeuropa in der Feudalzeit', *Jahrbuch für die Geschichte der sozialistischen Länder Europas*, xxi (no. 2, 1977), 115–30; V. Press, 'Französische Volkserhebungen und deutsche Agrarkonflikte zwischen dem 16. und dem 18. Jahrhundert', *Beiträge zur historischen Sozialkunde*, vii (1977) 76–81; and the articles in G. Heckenast (ed.), *Aus der Geschichte der ostmitteleuropäischen Bauernbewegungen im 16.–17. Jahrhundert* (Budapest, 1977). See also E. Le Roy Ladurie, 'Peasants', in P. Burke (ed.), *The New Cambridge Modern History*, Vol. xiii, companion volume (Cambridge, 1979), pp. 115–63, for the revolts pp. 137 f., and Y.-M. Bercé *Révoltes et révolutions dans L'Europe moderne (XVIe – XVIIIe siècles)* (Paris, 1980). The papers presented to a conference on early modern European peasant movements held in Bochum (1980) are now available in W. Schulze (ed.), *Aufstände, Revolten und Prozesse: Beiträge zu bäuerlichen Widerstandsbewegungen im frühneuzeitlichen Europa* (Stuttgart, 1983). The most recent attempt to survey the history of revolts and early modern revolution is P. Zagorin, *Rebels and Rulers 1500 to 1660*, 2 vols (Cambridge, 1982).

6 M. Bloch, *Caractères originaux de l'histoire rurale française*, Vol. i (Paris, 1952), p. 175.

7 L. von Ranke, *Deutsche Geschichte im Zeitalter der Reformation*, ed. P. Joachimsen, Vol. ii (Meersburg and Leipzig, 1933), p. 126.

8 C. Hill, 'The many-headed monster in late Tudor and early Stuart political thinking', in C. H. Carter (ed.), *From the Renaissance to the Counter-*

Reformation: Essays in Honour of G. Mattingly (New York, 1965), pp. 296–324, and Claude Malingre, *Troisieme tome de l'histoire de nostre temps ou suite de l'histoire des guerres contre les rebelles de France, ez années 1623 et 1624* (Paris, 1624), p. 522.

9 J. H. Elliott, 'Revolution and continuity in early modern Europe', *Past and Present*, xlii (1969) 35–56, here 40.

10 J. C. G. H., *Gedanken über die gegenwärtigen Unruhen in Deutschland* (1785), pp. 26 ff.

11 See my statements in *Bäuerlicher Widerstand* (as in n. 3), pp. 21 ff.

12 Y.-M. Bercé, *Croquants et Nu-Pieds* (as in n. 2), p. 49, stresses the duration of more than one day and the participation of several villages. See also G. Heitz and G. Vogler, 'Bauernbewegungen in Europa vom 16. bis zum 18. Jahrhundert', in Heitz and Vogler, *Agrarfrage und bürgerliche Revolutionen beim Übergang vom Feudalismus zum Kapitalismus* (Rostock, 1980), pp. 3–21, esp. pp. 4 f., which contain criteria for the definition of historical phenomena as 'peasant movements'. It is argued here that peasant movements arise spontaneously, but always show signs of a certain degree or organisation.

13 For this question, see W. Schulze (ed.), *Aufstände, Revolten* (as in n. 5). The question of resistance by litigation has not yet been sufficiently examined. For France see now the remarks by J. P. Gutton, *La Sociabilité villageoise dans l'ancienne France: solidarités et voisinages du XVIe au XVIIIe siècle* (Paris, 1979), pp. 123 ff. and 155 ff. and, as an example of detailed research, Y. Castan, 'Attitudes et motivations dans les conflicts entre seigneurs et communautés devant le Parlement de Toulouse au XVIIIe siècle', *Annales des lettres de Nice* (1969), 233–9. For England, see J. Brewer and J. Styles (eds), *An Ungovernable People: the English and their Law in the Seventeenth and Eighteenth Centuries* (London, 1980).

14 G. R. Elton, *England under the Tudors*, 2nd edn (London, 1974), p. 59. Some examples can be found in R. B. Manning, 'Patterns of violence in early Tudor enclosure riots', *Albion*, vi (1974), 120–33, and in Manning, 'Violence and social conflict in mid-Tudor rebellions', *Journal of British Studies*, xvi (1977), 18–40; B. Sharp, *In Contempt of All Authority: Rural Artisans and Riot in the West of England 1580–1660* (Berkeley, Calif., 1980), and P. Clark, *English Provincial Society from the Reformation to the Revolution: Religion, Politics and Society in Kent, 1500–1640* (Hassocks, 1977), pp. 78 ff., and Clark, 'Popular protest and disturbances in Kent', *Economic History Review*, xxix (1976), 365–82. J. Goring, 'The riot at Bayham Abbey, June 1525', *Sussex Archaeological Collections*, cxvi (1978), 1–10.

15 The research project of Dr F. Ranieri, from the Max-Planck Institute for Legal History in Frankfurt should be mentioned here. Dr Ranieri concentrates on a systematic examination of lawsuits brought before the Imperial Supreme Court (*Reichskammergericht*).

16 B. F. Poršnev, 'Formen und Wege des bäuerlichen Kampfes gegen die feudale Ausbeutung', *Sowjetwissenschaft GA* (1952), 440–59. This thesis is applied to German territories especially by G. Heitz, 'Der Zusammenhang zwischen den Bauernbewegungen und der Entwicklung des Absolutismus in Mitteleuropa', *Zeitschrift für Geschichtswissenschaft*, Sonderheft, xiii (1965), 71–83. Poršnev

himself tried to show this connection in the French revolts preceding the *Fronde*, see his *Die Volksaufstände in Frankreich vor der Fronde 1623–1648* (Leipzig, 1954), pp. 239 f.

17 J. A. Kosminski, 'Das Problem des Klassenkampfes in der Epoche des Feudalismus', *Sowjetwissenschaft GSR* (1952), 460–82, here 466. See also L. Yaresh, 'The peasant wars in Soviet historiography', *American Slavic and East Europe Review*, xvi (1957), 241–59.

18 This seems to apply in particular to the research carried out in the German Democratic Republic. See the various articles by G. Heitz *et al.* (eds), *Der Bauer im Klassenkampf* (Berlin-East, 1975). The last quotation is from B. Töpfer, 'Volksbewegungen, Ideologie und gesellschaftlicher Fortschritt in der Epoche des entwickelten Feudalismus', *Zeitschrift für Geschichtswissenschaft*, xxv (1977), 1158–67. See also C. Bobinska, 'Propriété féodale et luttes paysannes en Pologne méridionale', *Annales historiques de la Révolution française*, xxvi (1974), 279–93, and A Maczak, 'Polnische Forschungen auf dem Gebiete der Agrargeschichte des 16. und 17. Jahrhunderts (1945–1957)', *Acta Poloniae Historica*, i (1958), 33–57, and Maczak, 'La paysannerie et les luttes des classes', ibid., xvi (1967), 139–47.

19 R. Hilton, *Bond Men Made Free: Medieval Peasant Movements and the English Rising of 1381* (London, 1973), p. 11. See especially J. H. Elliott's convincing statement in 'Revolution and continuity' (as in n. 9), 42: 'But it is one thing to establish the existence of social antagonisms, and another to assume that they are the principal cause of conflict.'

20 See especially R. Mousnier, *Peasant Uprisings in Seventeenth Century France, Russia and China* (London, 1971), pp. 3 ff., as an example of a similar interpretation of different aspects of his own earlier work. See also a recent article by G. Rudé, who realises that Marxist theory does not account adequately for the ideology of popular protest. Rudé proposes a new model of this ideology as consisting of 'inherent' and 'derived' elements: G. Rudé, 'L'idéologie de la contestation populaire á l'époque pré-industrielle', *Europa: Revue d'étude interdisciplinaire*, iii (1979) 7–17.

21 B. F. Poršnev (as in n. 16). The French translation of his book did not appear until 1963. A German translation was published in 1954. For a first and cursory survey of his views in English, see Poršnev, 'The legend of the seventeenth century in French history', *Past and Present*, viii (1955), 15–27.

22 See the following works: R. Mandrou, *Classes et luttes de classes en France au début du XVIIe siècle* (Messina and Florence, 1965); J. H. M. Salmon, 'Venality of office and popular sedition in seventeenth century France: a review of a controversy', *Past and Present*, xxxvii (1967), 21–43; C. Vivanti, 'Le rivolte popolare in Francia prima della Fronde e la crisi del secolo XVII', *Rivista Storica Italiana*, lxxvi (1964), 957–81; R. Mandrou, 'Vingt ans après, ou une direction de recherches fécondes: les révoltes populaires en France au XVIIe siècle', *Revue Historique*, ccxlii (1969), 29–40. See the last comment on this much debated topic by L. Lavallée, 'Les soulèvements populaires en France dans la première moitié du 17e siècle: Etat de la question', *Histoire sociale – Social History*, x (1977), 427–32.

23 The following publications in particular should be mentioned: Y.-M. Bercé, *Histoire des Croquants: Etude des soulèvements populaires au 17e siècle dans le*

sudouest de la France, 2 vols (Geneva, 1974); M. Foisil, *La Révolte des Nu-pieds et les révoltes normandes de 1639* (Paris, 1970); R. Pillorget, *Les Mouvements insurrectionels de Provence entré 1596 et 1715* (Paris, 1975). For comments on an exclusively anti-fiscalist approach, see J. H. M. Salmon, *Society in Crisis: France in the Sixteenth Century* (London, 1975), pp. 276 ff. and Salmon, 'Peasant revolt in Vivarais, 1575-1580', *French Historical Studies*, xi (1979), 1-28.

24 See, for example, D. Sabean, 'Markets, uprisings and leadership in peasant societies' (see n. 5); Sabean, 'The communal basis of pre-1800 peasant uprisings in Western Europe', *Comparative Politics* (1976), 355-64, and C. Tilly, 'Major forms of collective action in Western Europe 1500-1975', *Theory and Society*, iii (1976), 365-75.

25 C. S. L. Davies, 'Peasant revolt in France and England: a comparison', *Agricultural History Review*, xxi (1973), 122-34.

26 Y.-M. Bercé, *Croquants et Nu-pieds* (see n. 2); C. Tilly, 'Major forms of collective action' (see n. 24). The same problem is dealt with by J. Blum, 'The European village as a community: origins and functions', *Agricultural History*, xlv (1971), 155-78. For the region east of the Elbe, see H. Harnisch, 'Landgemeinde, feudalherrlich-bäuerliche Klassenkämpfe und Agrarverfassung im Spätfeudalismus', *Zeitschrift für Geschichtswissenschaft*, xxvi (1978), 887-97.

27 Tilly's distinction does not seem to be quite clear. 'Reactive' protest against exaggerated labour services naturally can be explained as a 'proactive' measure.

28 See J. Petran, 'Der Höhepunkt der Bewegungen der untertänigen Bauern in Böhmen', *Acta Universitatis Carolinae – Philosophica et Historica*, iii (1969), 122, and R. Mandrou, 'Vingt ans après (as in n. 22), 40. However, Mandrou's notion of 'blind power' (*force aveugle*) differs from that used by Poršnev.

29 See, for example, E. P. Thompson, 'The moral economy of the English crowd in the eighteenth century', *Past and Present*, l (1971), 76-131, and G. Rudé, *The Crowd in History: a Study of Popular Disturbances in France and England 1730-1848* (New York and London, 1964).

30 N. Z. Davis, Society and Culture in Early Modern France, (London, 1974), p. 154.

31 See, for example, J. Cornwall, *The Revolt of the Peasantry 1549* (London, 1977), p. 238.

32 G. Duby, *Les Trois Ordres ou l'imaginaire du féodalisme* (Paris, 1978).

33 Convincingly described by K. Eder, *Glaubensspaltung und Landstände in Österreich ob der Enns, 1525-1602* (Linz, 1936), and in more detail by H. Sturmberger, *Georg Erasmus Tschernembl: Religion, Libertät und Widerstand* (Graz, 1953). For France see the results presented by M. Foisil, *La Révolte des Nu-Pieds et les Révoltes Normandes de 1639* (Paris, 1970), pp. 339 f.

34 Unfortunately this problem has not been dealt with satisfactorily by international research on estates and representative assemblies, although E. Lousse, 'Gouvernés et gouvernants en Europe occidentale durant le bas moyen âge et les temps modernes', *Standen en Landen*, xxxv (1966) 7-48, here 43, has drawn attention to it. See also R. Mousnier, 'La participation des gouvernés à l'activité des gouvernants dans la France du XVIIe et du XVIIIe siècle', in *Gouvernés et Gouvernants*, vol. iii, Recueils de la Société Jean Bodin, vol. xxiv (Brussels, 1966), pp. 235-97, reprinted in Mousnier, *La Plume, la Faucille et le*

Marteau (Paris, 1970), pp. 231-62. A first attempt of my own is W. Schulze, 'Die politische Bedeutung des gemeinen Mannes in ständischen Versammlungen des 16. Jahrhunderts', *Zeitschrift für Agrargeschichte und Agrarsoziologie*, xxi (1973), 48-64.

35 See the articles published in the journal *Standen en Landen* and in *Studies presented to the International Commission for the history of parliamentary assemblies/Etudes presentées à la commission internationale pour l'histoire des assemblées d'états.* See also the new journal covering this field of research, *Parliaments, Estates and Representation*, i (1981).

36 The problem is sketched by P. Kriedte, H. Medick and J. Schlumbohm, *Industrialisierung vor der Industrialisierung: Gewerbliche Warenproduktion auf dem Land in der Formationsperiode des Kapitalismus* (Göttingen, 1977), pp. 26 ff.

37 E. Hobsbawm, 'Agriculture et capitalisme en Ecosse au XVIIIe siècle: les réformateurs écossais au 18e siècle', *Annales ESC*, xxxiii (1978), 580-601.

38 The debate in the early 1950s which followed the publication of M. Dobb, *Studies in the Development of Capitalism* (London, 1946) has been republished and is discussed in R. Hilton's introduction to P. Sweezy, M. Dobb *et al.*, *The Transition from Feudalism to Capitalism* (London, 1976). The new debate has been initiated by R. Brenner, 'Agrarian class structure and economic development in pre-industrial Europe', *Past and Present*, lxx (1976), 30-75. Some comments on Brenner appeared in *Past and Present*, lxxviii-lxxx and lxxxv.

39 D. Pennington in a short contribution to a discussion at a conference on seventeenth-century revolutions held in London. See the conference report in *Past and Present*, xiii (1958), 64.

40 E. Le Roy Ladurie, 'Über die Bauernaufstände in Frankreich 1548-1648', in *Wirtschaftliche and soziale Strukturen im säkularen Wandel: Festschrift für W. Abel zum 70. Geburtstag*, Vol. i (Hanover, 1974), pp. 277-305, and Ladurie, 'Révoltes et contestations rurales en France de 1675 à 1788', *Annales ESC*, xxix (1974), 6-22; Y.-M. Bercé, *Croquants et Nu-Pieds* (as in n. 2), pp. 47-58.

41 See L. Accati, '"Vive le Roi sans taille et sans gabelle": Una discussione sulle rivolte contadine', *Quaderni Storici*, vii (1972), 1071-103.

42 E. Le Roy Ladurie, 'Über die Bauernaufstände', and his 'Révoltes' (as in n. 40). See also Y.-M. Bercé, *Croquants et Nu-Pieds* (as in n. 2), pp. 56. f., and his 'Überlegungen zu den französischen Bauernrevolten des 16. bis 18 Jahrhunderts', in W. Schulze (ed.), *Aufstände, Revolten* (as in n. 5). A relatively cautious answer regarding the waning of peasant rebellions in the seventeenth century is given by P. Goubert, *La vie quotidienne des paysans français au XVIIe siècle* (Paris, 1982), pp. 272-90.

43 For an overview, see the article by C. S. L. Davies (as in n. 25), and Davies, 'Les révoltes populaires en Angleterre (1500-1700)', *Annales ESC*, xxiv (1969), 24-60. A. Fletcher, *Tudor Rebellions*, 2nd edn (London, 1973). For the most recent results of research on this question see A. B. Appleby, 'Common land and peasant unrest in sixteenth century England: a comparative note', *Peasant Studies Newsletter*, iv (1975), 20-3; J. Cornwall, *Revolt of the Peasantry* (London, 1977); S. K. Land, *Kett's Rebellion: the Norfolk Rising of 1549* (Ipswich, 1977); R. B. Manning, 'The rebellions of 1549 in England', (review article), *Sixteenth Century Journal*, x (1979), 93-9, and D. MacCulloch, 'Kett's rebellion in

context', *Past and Present*, lxxxiv (1979), 36–59. D. M. Loades, *Politics and the Nation 1450–1660: Obedience, Resistance and Public Order* (London, 1974) used the concepts of resistance and public order for an interpretation of English history during the period covered here.

44 See the diverging positions of R. H. Tawney, *The Agrarian Problem in the Sixteenth Century* (London, 1912), and E. Kerridge, *Agrarian Problems in the 16th Century and after* (London and New York, 1969). For an up-to-date summary, see B. A. Holderness, *Pre-Industrial England: Economy and Society from 1500 to 1750* (London, 1976), esp. pp. 45 ff., and W. G. Hoskins, *The Age of Plunder: the England of Henry VIII, 1500–1547* (London, 1976), pp. 53 ff.

45 L. A. Tilly, 'The food riot as a form of political conflict in France', *Journal of Interdisciplinary History*, ii (1971/2), 23–57; R. B. Rose, 'Eighteenth century price riots and public policy in England', *International Review of Social History*, vi (1961), 277–92, and J. Stevenson, 'Food riots in England, 1792–1818', in R. Quinault and J. Stevenson (eds), *Popular Protest and Public Order* (London, 1974), pp. 33–74. See M. Beloff, *Public Order and Popular Disturbances 1660–1714* (Oxford, 1938), (repr. 1963), for a survey of government policy towards disturbances at the end of the seventeenth century.

46 V. Buganov, 'Bauernaufstände und Bauernkriege in Ost-, Mittel- und Westeuropa in der Feudalzeit', *Jahrbuch für die Geschichte der sozialistischen Länder Europas*, xxi (no. 2, 1977), 115–30, here 119. For the earlier period, see Buganov, 'Sozialstruktur und Klassenkampf der Bauern im feudalen Rußland (9.–16. Jahrhundert)', *Jahrbuch für Wirtschaftsgeschichte*, (no. 1, 1980), 101–15.

47 See J. Petran's article cited in n. 28.

48 Y.-M. Bercé, *Révoltes et Révolutions* (as in n. 5), pp. 172 f., distinguishes three phases of revolt: first the 'resistance of east-European peasants to the second serfdom during the sixteenth and seventeenth centuries', followed by 'the opposition against centralisation in the west-European kingdoms', characteristic for the seventeenth century, and last 'the troubles accompanying the waning of the manorial system in the eighteenth century'.

49 The older state of research was summed up by O. Schiff, 'Die deutschen Bauernaufstände von 1525 bis 1789', *Historische Zeitschrift*, cxxx (1924), 189–209, and G. Franz, *Geschichte des deutschen Bauernstandes vom frühen Mittelalter bis zum 19. Jahrhundert*, 2nd edn (Stuttgart, 1976), pp. 179–98. For a generally similar argument, see K. Gerteis, 'Regionale Bauernrevolten zwischen Bauernkrieg und Französischer Revolution: Eine Bestandsaufnahme', *Zeitschrift für Historische Forschung*, vi (1979), pp. 37–62. The most recent state of research is summed up by P. Bierbrauer, 'Bäuerliche Revolten in Alten Reich: Ein Forschungsbericht', in P. Blickle (ed.), *Aufruhr und Empörung? Studien zum bäuerlichen Widerstand im Alten Reich* (Munich, 1980), pp. 1–68. For research in the GDR, see the relevant chapters in M. Steinmetz, *Deutschland 1476–1648* (Berlin-East, 1967), pp. 254 ff., and 358 ff., and G. Schilfert, *Deutschland 1648–1789*, 3rd edn (Berlin-East, 1975), pp. 25 ff., 85 ff. and 141 ff. In addition, see H. Schultz, 'Bäuerliche Klassenkämpfe zwischen frühbürgerlicher Revolution und Dreißigjährigem Krieg', *Zeitschrift für Geschichtswissenschaft*, xx (1972), 157–73, and the bibliographical list compiled by I. Volz and H.-S. Brather, 'Der deutsche Bauer im Klassenkampf (1470–1648): Auswahlbibliographie der

Veröffentlichungen in den sozialistischen Staaten aus den Jahren 1945 bis 1972', in G. Heitz *et al.* (eds), *Der Bauer im Klassenkampf,* (as in n. 18), pp. 573–600

50 See for instance H. Holborn, *Deutsche Geschichte in der Neuzeit*, Vol. i: 'Das Zeitalter der Reformation und des Absolutismus' (Stuttgart, 1960), pp. 56–68, 162–5, 370–2. The remarks by R. Brenner in his article cited in n. 38, esp. 53 f., illustrate this tendency.

51 There are many literary reflections of this. Some territorial princes made comparisons between the great peasant war and the peasant revolts in their own territories in the late sixteenth century. A local leader, for example, was called 'Thomas Münzer' by Christof von Waldburg. See W. Kröger, 'Bauernkrieg und Literatur: Fragestellungen in der Erforschung der literarischen Rezeption des deutschen Bauernkriegs', *Daphnis*, vi (1977), 273–90, and E. Schäfer, 'Der deutsche Bauernkrieg in der neulateinischen Literatur', *Daphnis*, ix (1980), 1–31.

52 See the documentary evidence in W. Schulze, *Bäuerlicher Widerstand* (as in n. 3), pp. 167 f.

53 For a more extensive version of what is presented here as a short summary, see ibid., pp. 49 ff. The references below include only new literature and quotations.

54 See K. Eder, *Glaubensspaltung und Landstände in Österreich ob der Enns, 1525–1602* (Linz, 1936), p. 231.

55 For this revolt, see the recent dissertation by G. Gentsch, *Der Klassenkampf der ländlichen Untertanen im Erzgebirge und Vogtland im 17. Jahrhundert*, phil. diss (PH Dresden, 1977).

56 This calculation is based on printed material and on archival research carried out by colleagues and my research team. For the period 1648–1789, see the article by W. Troßbach on 'Bauernbewegungen in deutschen Kleinterritorien', in W. Schulze (ed.), *Aufstände, Revolten* (as in n. 5).

57 See the new studies by V. Press, 'Der hohenzollern-hechingische Landesvergleich von 1788: Reichsrecht und Untertanenvertretung im Zeichen der Französischen Revolution', *Zeitschrift für Hohenzollernsche Geschichte*, xiv (1978), 77–108, and Press, 'Von den Untertanenrevolten des 16. zur konstitutionellen Verfassung des 19. Jahrhunderts: Die Untertanenkonflikte in Hohenzollern-Hechingen und ihre Lösungen', in H. Weber (ed.), *Politische Ordnungen und soziale Kräfte im Alten Reich* (Wiesbaden, 1980), pp. 85–112.

58 K. S. von Galera, *Die Riedesel zu Eisenbach*, Vol. v (Neustadt a. d. Aich, 1961), pp. 253 ff. For the confrontations in this region in the seventeenth century, see G. Schmidt, 'Agrarkonflikte im Riedeselischen Gericht Moos im 17. Jahrhundert', in *Archiv für hessische Geschichte und Altertumskunde*, Neue Folge, xxxvii (1979), 215–328.

59 See J. Jacquart's summary in G. Duby and A. Wallon (eds), *Histoire de la France rurale*, Vol. ii, (Paris, 1975), pp. 329 ff., earlier confirmed by F. Hincker, *Les Francais devant l'impôt* (Paris, 1971), pp. 64 ff.

60 See now C. Ulbrich, 'Bäuerlicher Widerstand in Triberg' in P. Blickle (ed.), *Aufruhr und Empörung?* (as in n. 49), pp. 146–214.

61 I would like to cite particularly *Merkwürdige Reichs-Hof-Raths-Conclusa*, 4 pts (Frankfurt/M., 1762–8), and J. U. von Cramer, *Wetzlarische Nebenstunden, worinnen auserlesene beym höchstpreislichen Cammergericht entschiedene Rechtshändel ...*, 128 pts (Ulm, 1775–83; general index: 1779).

62 See R. Lehmann, *Quellen zur Lage der Privatbauern in der Niederlausitz im Zeitalter des Absolutismus* (Berlin, 1957).

63 This concept is borrowed from G. Oestreich, 'Standetum und Staatsbildung in Deutschland', in Oestreich, *Geist und Gestalt des frühmodernen Staates* (Berlin, 1969), pp. 277–89, here p. 279 and pp. 285 ff.

64 V. Press hints at this issue in 'Von den Untertanenrevolten' (as in n. 57), esp. 88 and 98 f., and Press, 'Die aufgeschobene Mediatisierung: Finanzkrise der Kleinstaaten und kaiserliche Stabilisierungspolitik', in *Bericht über die 32. Versammlung deutscher Historiker in Hamburg, 4. bis 8. Oktober 1978* (Stuttgart, 1979), pp. 139–41.

65 See W. Schulze, *Bäuerlicher Widerstand* (as in n. 3), pp. 128 ff., and V. Press, 'Von den Untertanenrevolten' (as in n. 57), 103 ff., on the authority of the emperor, which should not be underrated as far as the peasant revolts of this period are concerned.

66 As in the case of the community of Böhmenkirch in 1580, documented in W. Schulze, *Bäuerlicher Widerstand* (as in n. 3), pp. 173 ff.

67 Bayerisches Staatsarchiv Neuburg, Lehen und Adel 2913 I, II.

68 For some examples, see W. Schulze, *Bäuerlicher Widerstand* (as in n. 3), p. 135, and doc. no. 24, pp. 227 ff.

69 See E. Wolf, *Peasant Wars of the Twentieth Century* (London, 1971), p. 230.

70 Apart from the literature cited in n. 34, see the most recent comment on this question in H. Sturmberger, 'Der oberösterreichische Bauernaufstand von 1626 im Rahmen der Landesgeschichte', in *Der oberösterreichische Bauernkrieg* (Linz, 1976), pp. 1 ff., and Sturmberger, *Adam Graf Herberstorff: Herrschaft und Freiheit im konfessionellen Zeitalter* (Munich, 1976), pp. 259–308.

71 S. Riezler, 'Der Aufstand der bayerischen Bauern im Winter 1633 auf 1634', *Sitzungsberichte der bayerischen Akademie der Wissenschaften* (Phil.-Hist. Klasse, 1900), 33–95, and C. Probst, *Lieber bayrisch sterben: Der bayerische Volksaufstand der Jahre 1705 und 1706* (Munich, 1978), particularly pp. 122 ff. The numerous agrarian conflicts in Bavaria between 1400 and 1800 are analysed by R. Blickle, 'Agrarische Konflikte und Eigentumsordnung in Altbayern, 1400–1800', in W. Schulze (ed.), *Aufstände, Revolten und Prozesse*, (as in n. 5), pp. 166–87.

72 See W. Schulze, 'Zur veränderten Bedeutung sozialer Konflikte im 16. und 17. Jahrhundert', in H. U. Wehler (ed.), *Der Deutsche Bauernkrieg 1524–26*, Geschichte und Gesellschaft, Sonderheft, no. 1 (Göttingen, 1975), pp. 277–302, and W. Schulze, *Bäuerlicher Widerstand* (as in n. 3), pp. 76 ff.

73 J. H. Schmauss, *Academische Vorlesungen und Reden über das deutsche Staatsrecht*, ed. J. A. Heldmann (Lemgo, 1766), p. 665, and C. E. Weise, *Über die Berichterstattung auf Klagen deutscher Untertanen gegen ihre Landesherren an den höchsten Reichsgerichten* (Wetzlar, 1791), p. 9. J. L. E. Graf v. Barth-Barthenheim, *Das politische Verhältnis der verschiedenen Gattungen von Obrigkeiten zum Bauernstand im Erzherzogtum Österreich nieder der Enns*, Vol. i (Vienna, 1818), p. 42, stated that the peasant war meant a 'forcible warning not to drive the peasants to despair'.

74 See G. Bonis, 'Die Retorsionsgesetze von 1514', in G. Heckenast (ed.), *Aus der Geschichte der ostmitteleuropäischen Bauernbewegungen* (as in n. 5), pp. 309–16.

75 It is clear that the rebellions of 1548/9 put an end to Protector Somerset's social

policy, which was favourable towards the peasants. See M. L. Bush, *The Government Policy of Protector Somerset* (London, 1975), pp. 89 ff., and regarding the judicial possibilities open to the peasants W. R. D. Jones, *The Mid-Tudor Crisis 1539–1563* (London, 1973), pp. 116 ff.

76 See W. Schulze, *Bäuerlicher Widerstand*, p. 80 and the references to parallel territorial developments, ibid., pp. 106 ff.

77 See W. Schulze, 'Zur veränderten Bedeutung' (as in n. 72), p. 283.

78 For references to relevant studies, see ibid., pp. 293 ff. For England, see C. Hill, 'The many-headed monster' (as in n. 8), and for the middle of the sixteenth century, W. Zeeveld, *Foundations of Tudor Policy* (London, 1969), esp. pp. 190 ff., and Jones, *The Mid-Tudor Crisis* (as in n. 75), pp. 139 ff. There are no comparable investigations for France.

79 The literature on eighteenth-century German feudal law has not yet attracted special attention. For France see J. Q. C. Mackrell, *The Attack on 'Feudalism' in Eighteenth-Century France* (London and Toronto, 1973). Some references to this interesting material can be found in K. S. Bader, 'Dorf und Dorfgemeinde im Zeitalter von Naturrecht und Aufklärung', in *Festschrift für K. G. Hugelmann*, Vol. i (Aalen, 1959), pp. 1–36.

80 This term is taken from A. W. Ertel, *Praxis aurea de jurisdictione civile et bassa, vulgo von der Niedergerichtsbarkeit* (Nuremberg, 1713), book ii, pp. 1 ff. It designates the possibility of 'legitimate resistance' based on the feudal law and its interpretation since the sixteenth century. The 'rebellio licita' had already been acknowledged by J. Althusius in cases where the existence of an authority's subject was threatened. See W. Schulze, 'Der bäuerliche Widerstand und die "Rechte der Menschheit"', in G. Birtsch (ed.), *Zur Geschichte der Grund- und Freiheitsrechte vom Ausgang des Mittelalters bis zur Revolution von 1848* (Göttingen, 1981), pp. 41–56, and W. Schulze, 'Herrschaft und Widerstand in der Sicht des "gemeinen Mannes" im 16. und 17. Jahrhundert', in H. Mommsen und W. Schulze (eds), *Vom Elend der Handarbeit* (Stuttgart, 1981), pp. 182–98, where this question is analysed in more detail.

81 E. P. Thompson, 'Moral economy' (as in n. 29).

82 See W. Schulze, 'Herrschaft und Widerstand' (as in n. 80).

83 Rodney Hilton also opposes this very popular interpretation. See his *Bond Men Made Free* (as in n. 19), p. 234.

84 J. Jacquart, 'L'échec des résistances paysannes', in G. Duby and A. Wallon (eds), *Histoire de la France rurale*, Vol. ii (Paris, 1975), p. 329.

85 J. H. Elliott, 'Revolution and continuity in early modern Europe', *Past and Present*, xlii (1969), 35–56. Elliott seems to be convinced that only movements 'from above' were capable of leading to a 'mutation in the state' (p. 52), although he is aware of the parallel problem of socially motivated manifestations of discontent.

86 ibid., 45.

87 This seems to be the general impression of research in recent years. Cf. the quotation from N. Z. Davis above, p. 69.

88 Y.-M. Bercé, *Histoire des Croquants* (as in n. 2), Vol. ii, pp. 546 and 577.

89 See the bishop's letter to the emperor from 1580, printed in J. W. Hoffmann, *Sammlung ungedruckter und zu den Geschichten auch Staats-Lehn- und anderen*

Rechten des Heiligen Römischen Reiches gehöriger Nachrichten: Documenten und Urkunden (Halle, 1736), pp. 568 ff.

90 J. Blum, *The End of the Old Order in Rural Europe* (Princeton, NJ, 1978), p. 353.

91 F. Bacon, 'Of seditions and troubles', in J. Spedding (ed.), *The Works of Francis Bacon*, Vol. vi (London, 1861), pp. 406–12. cf. T. K. Rabb, 'Francis Bacon and the reform of society', in Rabb and J. E. Seigel (eds), *Action and Conviction in Early Modern History: Essays in Memory of E. H. Harbison* (Princeton, NJ, 1969), pp. 169–93.

92 J. J. Becher, *Politische Discurs* (Frankfurt, 1688), p. 37.

93 The quotation is from D. Silagi, *Ungarn und der geheime Mitarbeiterkreis Kaiser Leopolds II.* (Munich, 1961) p. 119.

94 cf. A. Fischel, 'Christian Julius Schierl von Schierendorf. Vorläufer des liberalen Zentralismus im Zeitalter Josefs I. und Karls VI.' in Fischel, *Studien zur österreichischen Reichsgeschichte* (Vienna, 1906), pp. 288–93, and H. J. Bidermann, *Geschichte der österreichischen Gesamtstaatsidee 1526–1804*, pt ii (Innsbruck, 1889), p. 39, and nn. 48/49, pp. 186 ff.

95 A statement frequently made by late-sixteenth-century Upper German princes shocked by peasant revolts.

96 J. G. H. Justi, *Grundsätze der Policeywissenschaft*, 3rd edn (Göttingen, 1782), p. 312, who agrees with a point made by Frederick II, who obviously did not fear any more rebellions in his country, cf. G. B. Volz (ed.), *Werke Friedrichs des Großen*, Vol. vii (Berlin, 1913), p. 145.

97 cf. Rodney Hilton's statement that 'the concept of the free man, owing no obligation, not even deference, to an overlord, is one of the most important, if intangible legacies of the medieval peasant to the modern world', in Hilton, *Bond Men Made Free* (as in n. 19), p. 235.

98 H. G. Koenigsberger, 'Dominium regale or dominium politicum et regale? Monarchies and parliaments in early modern Europe', in K. Bosl (ed.), *Der moderne Parlamentarismus und seine Grundlagen in der ständischen Repräsentation* (Berlin, 1977), pp. 43–68.

Index